CREATURES
OF A DAY

ALSO BY IRVIN D. YALOM

CREATURES OF A DAY

And Other Tales of Psychotherapy

IRVIN D. YALOM

BASIC BOOKS
A Member of the Perseus Books Group
New York

Published by Basic Books,
A Member of the Perseus Books Group

Books published by Basic Books are available at special discounts for
bulk purchases in the United States by corporations, institutions,
and other organizations. For more information, please contact the
Special Markets Department at the Perseus Books Group, 2300
Chestnut Street, Suite 200, Philadelphia, PA 19103, or call (800)
810-4145, ext. 5000, or e-mail special.markets@perseusbooks.com.

Library of Congress Cataloging-in-Publication Data
Yalom, Irvin D., 1931–
    Creatures of a day : and other tales of psychotherapy / Irvin D.
Yalom Basic Books.
        pages   cm
    ISBN 978-0-465-02964-8 (hardcover) —
ISBN 978-0-465-04051-3 (e-book)
    1. Psychotherapy—Case studies.   2. Psychotherapist and
patient—Case studies.   I. Title.
    RC480.5.Y33 2014
    616.89'14—dc23

                                                    2014035737

10 9 8 7 6 5 4 3 2 1

To Marilyn,
my wife of sixty years, yet not long enough

CONTENTS

All of us are creatures of a day; the rememberer and the remembered alike. All is ephemeral—both memory and the object of memory. The time is at hand when you will have forgotten everything; and the time is at hand when all will have forgotten you. Always reflect that soon you will be no one, and nowhere.

—**Marcus Aurelius, *The Meditations***

~ 1 ~

The Crooked Cure

Dr. Yalom, I would like a consultation. I've read your novel,
When Nietzsche Wept, *and wonder if you'd be willing to
see a fellow writer with a writing block.*
—Paul Andrews

No doubt Paul Andrews sought to pique my interest with
his email. And he succeeded: I'd never turn away a fellow
writer. As for the writing block, I feel blessed by not having
been visited by one of those creatures and I was keen to help
him tackle it. Ten days later Paul arrived for his appointment. I
was startled by his appearance. For some reason I had expected
a frisky, tormented, middle-aged writer, yet entering my office
was a wizened old man, so stooped over that he appeared to be
scrutinizing the floor. As he inched slowly through my doorway, I wondered how he had possibly made it to my office at the
top of Russian Hill. Almost able to hear his joints creaking, I
took his heavy battered briefcase, held his arm, and guided him
to his chair.

1

"Thankee, thankee, young man. And how old are you?"

"Eighty years old," I answered.

"Ahhh, to be eighty again."

"And you? How many years do you have?"

"Eighty-four. Yes, that's right, *eighty-four*. I know that startles you. Most folks guess I'm in my thirties."

I took a good look at him, and for a moment our gazes locked. I felt charmed by his elfish eyes and the wisp of a smile playing on his lips. As we sat in silence for a few moments looking at one another, I imagined we basked in a glow of elder comradeship, as though we were travelers on a ship who, one cold foggy night, fell into conversation on the deck and discovered we had grown up in the same neighborhood. We instantly knew one another: our parents had suffered through the Great Depression, we had witnessed those legendary duels between DiMaggio and Ted Williams, and remembered rationing cards for butter and gasoline, and VE day, and Steinbeck's *Grapes of Wrath*, and Farrell's *Studs Lonigan*. No need to speak of any of this: we shared it all, and our bond felt secure. Now it was time to get to work.

"So Paul, if we may use first names—"

He nodded. "Of course."

"All I know about you comes from your short email. You wrote that you were a fellow writer, you've read my Nietzsche novel, and you have a writing block."

"Yes, and I'm requesting a single consultation. That's all. I'm on a fixed income and can't afford more."

"I'll do what I can. Let's start immediately and be as efficient as possible. Tell me what I should know about the block."

"If it's all right with you, I'll give you some personal history."

"That's fine."

"I have to go back to my grad school days. I was in philosophy at Princeton writing my doctorate on the incompatibility between Nietzsche's ideas on determinism and his espousal of self-transformation. But I couldn't finish. I kept getting distracted by such things as Nietzsche's extraordinary correspondence, especially by his letters to his friends and fellow writers like Strindberg. Gradually I lost interest altogether in his philosophy and valued him more as an artist. I came to regard Nietzsche as a poet with the most powerful voice in history, a voice so majestic that it eclipsed his ideas, and soon there was nothing for me to do but to switch departments and do my doctorate in literature rather than philosophy. The years went by, my research progressed well, but I simply could not write. Finally I arrived at the position that it was only through art that an artist could be illuminated, and I abandoned the dissertation project entirely and decided instead to write a novel on Nietzsche. But the writing block was neither fooled nor deterred by my changing projects. It remained as powerful and unmovable as a granite mountain. No progress was possible. And so it has continued until this very day."

I was stunned. Paul was eighty-four now. He must have begun working on his dissertation in his mid-twenties, *sixty years ago*. I had heard of professional students before, but sixty years? His life on hold for sixty years? No, I hoped not. It couldn't be.

"Paul, fill me in about your life since those college days."

"Not much to tell. Of course the university eventually decided I had stayed overtime, rang the bell, and terminated my student status. But books were in my blood, and I never strayed far from them. I took a job as a librarian at a state university, where I stayed put until retirement trying, unsuccessfully, to write all these years. That's it. That's my life. Period."

"Tell me more. Your family? The people in your life?"

Paul seemed impatient and spat his words out quickly: "No siblings. Married twice. Divorced twice. Mercifully short marriages. No children, thank God."

This is getting very odd, I thought. *So affable at first, Paul now seems intent on giving me as little information as possible. What's going on?*

I persevered. "Your plan was to write a novel about Nietzsche, and your email mentioned that you had read my novel *When Nietzsche Wept.* Can you say some more about that?"

"I don't understand your question."

"What feelings did you have about my novel?"

"A bit slow-going at first, but it gathered steam. Despite the stilted language and the stylized, improbable dialogue, it was, overall, not an unengrossing read."

"No, no, what I meant was your reaction to that novel appearing while you, yourself, were striving to write a novel about Nietzsche. Some feelings about that must have arisen."

Paul shook his head as though he did not wish to be bothered with that question. Not knowing what else to do, I continued on.

"Tell me, how did you get to me? Was my novel the reason you selected me for a consultation?"

"Well, whatever the reason, we're here now."

Things grow stranger by the minute, I thought. But if I were to offer him a useful consultation, I absolutely had to learn more about him. I turned to "old reliable," a question that never fails to provide heaps of information: "I need to know more about you, Paul. I believe it would help our work today if you'd take me through, in detail, a typical twenty-four-hour day in your life. Pick a day earlier this week, and let's start with your waking in the morning." I almost always ask this question in a consultation, as it provides invaluable information about so many areas of the patient's life—sleep, dreams, eating and work patterns—but most of all I learn how the patient's life is peopled.

Failing to share my investigative enthusiasm, Paul merely shook his head slightly as though to brush my question away. "There's something more important for us to discuss. For many years I had a long correspondence with my dissertation director, Professor Claude Mueller. You know his work?"

"Well, I'm familiar with his biography of Nietzsche. It's quite wonderful."

"Good. Very good. I'm exceptionally glad you think that," Paul said, as he reached into his briefcase and extracted a ponderous binder. "Well, I've brought that correspondence with me, and I'd like you to read it."

"When? You mean *now*?"

"Yes, there is nothing more important that we could do in this consultation."

I looked at my watch. "But we have only this one session, and reading this would take an hour or two, and it is so much more important that we—"

"Dr. Yalom, trust me, I know what I'm asking. Make a start. Please."

I was flummoxed. *What to do? He is absolutely determined. I've reminded him of our time constraints, and he is fully aware he has only this one meeting. On the other hand, perhaps Paul knows what he is doing. Perhaps he believes that this correspondence would supply all the information about him that I need. Yes, yes, the more I think about it, the more certain I am: this must be it.*

"Paul, I gather you're saying that this correspondence provides the necessary information about you?"

"If that assumption is necessary for you to read it, then the answer is yes."

Most unusual. An intimate dialogue is my profession, my home territory. It's where I am always comfortable and yet in this dialogue everything feels askew, out of joint. Maybe I should stop trying so hard and just go with the flow. After all, it's his hour. He's paying for my time. I felt a bit dizzy but acquiesced and held out my hand to accept the manuscript he proffered.

As Paul passed me the massive three-ring binder, he told me the correspondence extended over forty-five years and ended with Professor Mueller's death in 2002. I began by flipping the pages to familiarize myself with the project. Much care had gone into this binder. It seemed that Paul had saved, indexed, and dated everything that passed between them, both short casual notes and long discursive letters. Professor Mueller's letters were neatly typed with his small, exquisitely fashioned closing signature, while Paul's letters—both the early carbon copies and the later photocopies—ended simply with the letter *P*.

Paul nodded toward me. "Please start."

I read the first several letters and saw that this was a most urbane and engaging correspondence. Though Professor Mueller obviously had great respect for Paul, he chided him for his infatuation with wordplay. In the very first letter he said, "I see that you're in love with words, Mr. Andrews. You enjoy waltzing with them. But words are just the notes. It's the ideas that form the melody. It's the *ideas* that give our life structure."

"I plead guilty," retorted Paul in the ensuing letter. "I don't ingest and metabolize words, I love to dance with them. I greatly hope to be always guilty of this offense." A few letters later, despite the roles and the half century dividing them, they had dropped formal titles of Mister and Professor and used their first names, Paul and Claude.

In another letter, my eye fell on a statement written by Paul: "I never fail to perplex my companions." So I had company. Paul continued, "Hence, I shall always embrace solitude. I know I make the error of assuming that others share my passion for great words. I know I inflict my passions onto them. You can only imagine how all creatures flee and scatter when I approach them." *That sounds important*, I thought. *"Embracing solitude" is a nice cosmetic touch and puts a poetic spin on it, but I imagine he is a very lonely old man.*

And then, a couple of letters later, I had an "aha" moment when I came upon a passage that possibly offered the key to understanding this entire surreal consultation. Paul wrote, "So you see, Claude, what is there left for me but to look for the nimblest and noblest mind I can find. I need a mind likely to appreciate my sensibilities, my love of poetry, a mind incisive and bold enough to join me in dialogue. Do any of my words quicken your pulse, Claude? I need a light-footed partner for this dance. Would you do me the honor?"

A thunderclap of understanding burst in my mind. *Now I knew why Paul insisted I read the correspondence. It's so obvious. How had I missed it? Professor Mueller died twelve years ago, and Paul is now trolling for another dance partner! That's where my novel about Nietzsche comes in! No wonder I've been so confused. I thought I was interviewing him, whereas, in reality, he is interviewing me. That must be what is going on.*

I looked at the ceiling for a moment, wondering how to express this clarifying insight, when Paul interrupted my reverie by pointing to his watch and remarking, "Please, Dr. Yalom, our time passes. Please continue reading." I followed his wishes. The letters were compelling, and I gladly dived back into them.

In the first dozen letters there seemed a clear student-teacher relationship. Claude often suggested assignments, for example: "Paul, I'd like you to write a piece on comparing Nietzsche's misogyny with Strindberg's misogyny." I assumed Paul completed such assignments but saw no further mention of them in the correspondence. They must have discussed his assignments face to face. But gradually, halfway through the year, the teacher-student roles began to dissolve. There was little mention of assignments, and, at times, it was difficult to discern who was the teacher and who the pupil. Claude submitted several of his own poems seeking Paul's commentary, and Paul's responses were anything but deferential as he urged Claude to turn off his intellect and pay attention to his inner rush of feelings. Claude, on the other hand, critiqued Paul's poems for having passion but no intelligible content.

Their relationship grew more intimate and more intense with each exchange of letters. I wondered if I held in my hands the ashes of the great love, perhaps the only love, of Paul's life. *Maybe Paul is suffering from chronic unresolved grief. Yes, yes—certainly that's it. That's what he's trying to tell me by asking me to read these letters to and from the dead.*

As time went on I entertained one hypothesis after another, but in the end none offered the full explanation I sought. The more I read, the more my questions multiplied. Why had Paul come to see me? He labeled a writing block as his major problem, yet why did he show no interest whatsoever in exploring his writing block? Why did he refuse to give me details of his life? And why this singular insistence that I spend all our time together reading these letters of long ago? We needed to make sense of it. I resolved to broach all these issues with Paul before we parted.

Then I saw an exchange of letters that gave me pause. "Paul, your excessive glorification of sheer experience is veering in a dangerous direction. I must remind you, once again, of Socrates's admonition that the unexamined life is not worth living."

Good going, Claude! I silently rooted. *My point exactly. I identify entirely with your pressing Paul to examine his life.*

But Paul retorted sharply in his next letter, "Given the choice between living and examining, I'll choose living any day. I eschew the malady of explanation and urge you to do likewise. The drive to explain is an epidemic in modern thought and its major carriers are contemporary therapists: every shrink I have ever seen suffers from this malady, and it is addictive and contagious. Explanation is an illusion, a mirage, a construct, a soothing lullaby. Explanation has no existence. Let's call it by its proper name, a coward's defense against the white-knuckled, knee-knocking terror of the precariousness, indifference and capriciousness of sheer existence." I read this passage a second and third time and felt destabilized. My resolve to posit any of the ideas fermenting in my mind wavered. I knew that there was zero chance that Paul would accept *my* invitation to dance.

Every once in a while I looked up and saw Paul's eyes riveted on me, taking in my every reaction, signaling me to go on reading. But, finally, when I saw there were only ten minutes left, I closed the folder and firmly took charge.

"Paul, we've little time left, and I have several things I want to discuss with you. I'm uncomfortable because we're coming to the end of our session, and I've not really addressed the very reason you contacted me—your major complaint, your writing block."

"I never said that."

"But in your email to me you said . . . here, I have it printed out . . . " I opened my folder, but before I could locate it, Paul responded:

"I know my words: 'I would like a consultation. I've read your novel, *When Nietzsche Wept*, and wonder if you'd be willing to see a fellow writer with a writing block.'"

I looked up at him expecting a grin, but he was entirely serious. He *had* said he had a writing block but had not explicitly labeled it as the problem for which he wanted help. It was a word trap, and I fought back irritation at being trifled with. "I'm accustomed to helping folks with problems. That's what therapists do. So one can easily see why I made that assumption."

"I understand entirely."

"Well then, let's make a fresh start. Tell me, how can I be of help to you?"

"Your reflections on the correspondence?"

"Can you be more explicit? It would help me frame my comments."

"Any and every observation would be most helpful to me."

"All right." I opened the notebook and flipped through the pages. "As you know, I had time to read only a small portion, but overall I was captivated by it, Paul, and found it brimming with intelligence and erudition at the highest level. I was struck by the shift in roles. At first you were the student and he the teacher. But obviously you were a very special student, and within a few months this young student and this renowned professor corresponded as equals. There was no doubt he had the greatest respect for your comments and your judgments. He admired your prose, valued your critique of his work, and I can only imagine that the time and energy he gave to you must have far exceeded what he could possibly have provided the typical student. And, of course, given that the correspondence continued long after your tenure as a student, there is no doubt that you and he were immensely important to one another."

I looked at Paul. He sat motionless, his eyes filling with tears, eagerly drinking in all that I said, obviously thirsting for yet more. Finally, finally, we had had an encounter. Finally, I had given him something. I could bear witness to an event of extraordinary importance to Paul. I, and I alone, could testify that a great man deemed Paul Andrews to be significant. But the great man had died years ago, and Paul had now grown too frail to bear this fact alone. *He needed a witness, someone of stature,* and I had been selected to fill that role. Yes, I had no doubt of this. This explanation had the aroma of truth.

Now to convey some of these thoughts that would be of value to Paul. As I looked back on all my many insights and at the few minutes remaining to us, I was uncertain where to begin and ultimately decided to start with the most obvious: "Paul, what struck me most strongly about your correspondence was the intensity and the tenderness of the bond between you and Professor Mueller. It struck me as a deep love. His death must have been terrible for you. I wonder if that painful loss still lingers and *that* is the reason you desired a consultation. What do you think?"

Paul did not answer. Instead he held out his hand for the manuscript, and I returned it to him. He opened his briefcase, packed the binder of correspondence away, and zippered it shut.

"Am I right, Paul?"

"I desired a consultation with you because I desired it. And now I've had the consultation, and I obtained precisely what I wished for. You've been helpful, exceedingly helpful. I expected nothing less. Thank you."

"Before you leave, Paul, one more moment, please. I've always found it important to understand what helps. Could you expound for a moment on what you received from me? I believe that some greater clarification of this will serve you well in the future, and might be useful for me and my future clients."

"Irv, I regret having to leave you with so many riddles, but I'm afraid our time is up." He tottered as he tried to rise. I reached out and grabbed his elbow to steady him. Then he straightened himself, reached to shake my hand, and, with an invigorated gait, strode out of my office.

~ 2 ~

On Being Real

Charles, a personable business executive, had the right stuff behind him: a sterling education at Andover, Harvard, and Harvard Business School; a grandfather and father who were successful bankers; and a mother who was head of the board of trustees of an eminent women's college. And the right stuff around him: a San Francisco condo with a panoramic view from Golden Gate to the Bay Bridge; a lovely, socially prominent wife; a mid-six-figure salary; and a Jaguar XKE Convertible. And all of this at the advanced age of thirty-seven.

Yet he had no right stuff *inside*. Choked by self-doubts, recriminations, and guilt, Charles always perspired when he saw a police car on the highway. "Free-floating guilt searching for a sin—that's me," he joked. Moreover his dreams were relentlessly self-denigrating: he saw himself with large weeping wounds, cowering in a cellar or cave; he was a low-life, a lout, a criminal, a fake. But even as he demeaned himself in dreams, his quirky sense of humor shone through.

"I was waiting in a group of people who were auditioning for a role in a film," he told me, describing a dream in one of our early sessions. "I waited my turn and then performed my lines quite well. Sure enough, the director called me back from the waiting area and complimented me. He then asked about my previous film roles, and I told him I had never acted in a film. He slammed his hands on the table, stood up, and shouted as he walked out, 'You're no actor. You're impersonating an actor.' I ran after him shouting, 'If you impersonate an actor, you *are* an actor.' But he kept on walking and was now far in the distance. I screamed as loudly as I could, 'Actors impersonate people. That's what actors do!' But it was pointless. He had vanished, and I was alone."

Charles's insecurity seemed fixed and unaffected by any sign of worthiness. All positive things—accomplishments, promotions, and messages of love from wife, children, and friends; great feedback from clients or employees—passed quickly through him like water through a sieve. Even though we had, in my view, a good working relationship, he persisted in believing that I was impatient or bored with him. I once commented that he had holes in his pockets, and that phrase resonated so much that he repeated it often during our work. After hours of examining the sources of his self-contempt and scrutinizing all the usual suspects—lackluster IQ and SAT scores, failure to fight the elementary school bully, adolescent acne, awkwardness on the dance floor, occasional premature ejaculations, worries about the small size of his penis—we eventually arrived at the primal source of darkness.

"Everything bad began," Charles told me, "one morning when I was eight years old. My father, an Olympic sailor, set out on a gray windy day on his regular morning sail in a small boat from Bar Harbor, Maine, and never returned. That day is fixed in my mind: the horrendous family vigil, the growing angry storm, my mother's relentless pacing, our calls to friends and Coast Guard, our fixation on the telephone resting on the kitchen table with a red-checkered tablecloth, and our growing fear of the shrieking wind as nightfall approached. And worst of all was my mother's wailing early the next morning when the Coast Guard phoned with the news that they had found his empty boat floating upside down. My father's body was never found."

Tears streamed down Charles's cheeks, and emotion choked his voice as if the event had happened yesterday, rather than twenty-eight years ago. "That was the end of the good days, the end of my father's warm bear hugs and our games of horseshoes and Chinese checkers and Monopoly. I think I realized at the time that nothing would ever be the same."

Charles's mother mourned the rest of her life, and no one ever came along to replace his father. In his view, he became his own parent. Yes, being a self-made person had its good points: self-creation can be powerfully reaffirming. But it is lonely work, and often, in the dead of night, Charles ached for the warm hearth that had grown cold so long ago.

A year ago, at a charity event, Charles met James Perry, a high-tech entrepreneur. The two became friendly, and after several meetings, James offered Charles an attractive executive position in his new start-up. James, twenty years older, possessed the Silicon Valley golden touch, and though he had accumulated a vast fortune, he could not, as he put it, get out of the game, so he continued to launch new companies. Although their relation-

ship—friends, employer and employee, mentor and protégé—
was complex, Charles and James negotiated it with grace. Their
work required considerable travel, but whenever they were both
in town, they never failed to meet at the end of the day for drinks
and conversation. They talked about everything: the company,
the competition, new products, personnel problems, their fam-
ilies, investments, current movies, vacation plans, whatever
crossed their minds. Charles cherished those intimate meetings.

It was then, soon after meeting James, that Charles first contacted me. Paradoxical though it might seem to seek therapy
during a halcyon time of nurture and mentorship, there was a
ready explanation. The caring and fathering he received from
James stoked Charles's memory of his father's death and made
him more aware of what he had missed.

During our fourth month of therapy, Charles called to request an urgent meeting. He appeared in my office with an
ashen face. Walking slowly to his chair and lowering himself
carefully, he managed to utter two words, "He's dead."

"Charles, what happened?"

"James is dead. Massive stroke. Instant death. His widow
told me she'd had a dinner meeting with her board and came
home to find him slumped in a living room chair. Christ, he
hadn't even been sick! Totally, totally unexpected."

"How awful. What a shock this must be for you."

"How to describe it? I can't find the words. He was such
a good man, so kind to me. I was so privileged to know him.
I knew it! I knew all the while it was too good to last! Boy, I
really feel for his wife and kids."

"And I feel for you."

Over the next two weeks Charles and I met two to three times a week. He couldn't work, slept poorly, and wept often during our sessions. Again and again he expressed his respect for Perry and his deep gratitude for the time they had shared. The pain of past losses resurfaced, not only for his father but also his mother, now three years and one month dead. And for Michael, a childhood friend who died in the seventh grade, and for Cliff, a camp counselor, who died of a ruptured aneurism. Over and again Charles spoke of shock.

"Let's investigate your shock," I suggested. "What are its ingredients?"

"Death is always a shock."

"Keep going. Tell me about it."

"It's self-evident."

"Put it into words."

"Snap, life is gone. Just like that. There's no place to hide. There's no such thing as safety. Transiency . . . life is transient . . . I knew that. . . . Who doesn't? But I never thought much about it. Never wanted to think about it. But James's death makes me think of it. Forces me to, all the time. He was older, and I knew he'd die before me. It's just making me face things."

"Say more. What things?"

"About my own life. About my death that lies ahead. About the permanence of death. About being dead forever. Somehow that thought, *being dead forever*, has gotten stuck in my mind. Oh, I envy my Catholic friends and their afterlife stuff. I wish I could buy into that." He took a deep breath and looked up at me. "So *that's* what I've been thinking about. And also lots of questions about what's really important."

"Tell me about that."

"I think about the pointlessness of spending all my life at work and of making more money than I need. I've got enough now, but I keep on going. Just like James. I feel sad about the way I've lived. I could've been a better husband, a better father. Thank God there's still time."

Thank God there's still time. I welcomed that thought. I've known many who have managed to respond to grief in this positive fashion. The confrontation with the brute facts of life awakened them and catalyzed some major life changes. It looked as though that might be true for Charles, and I hoped to help him take that direction.

About three weeks after James Perry's death, however, Charles entered my office in a highly agitated state. He was breathing fast, and to calm himself, he put his hand to his chest and exhaled deeply as he slowly sank into his seat.

"I'm really glad we're meeting today. If we hadn't had this time scheduled, I probably would have phoned last night. I've just had one of the biggest shocks of my life."

"What happened?"

"Margot Perry, James's widow, phoned me yesterday to invite me over because she had something she wanted to talk about. I visited her last evening and . . . well, I'll get right to the point. Here's what she said: 'I didn't want to tell you this, Charles, but too many people know now, and I'd rather you hear it from me than from someone else. James did not die from a stroke. He committed suicide.' And since then I can't see straight. The world's turned upside down."

"How terrible for you! Tell me all that's going on inside."

"So much. A cyclone of feelings. It's hard to track."

"Start anywhere."

"Well, one of the first things that flashed in my mind is that *if he can commit suicide, then so can I.* I can't explain this any further except that I knew him so well and we were so close and he was like me and I was like him and, if he could do that, if he could kill himself, *then I can too.* That possibility shook the hell out of me. Don't worry—I'm not suicidal—but the thought lingers. *If he could, then so can I.* Death, suicide: they aren't abstract thoughts. Not any longer. They're real. And why? Why did he kill himself? I'll never find out. His wife is clueless, or pretends to be. She said she was totally caught by surprise. I'll have to get used to never knowing."

"Keep going, Charles. Tell me everything."

"The world is upside down. I don't know what's real anymore. He was so strong, so capable, so supportive of me. So caring, so thoughtful, and yet, think about it, at the same time he was making a cozy nest for me, he must have been so agonized he didn't want to exist any longer. What's real? What can you believe? All those times he was giving me support, giving me loving advice, at the same time he must have been contemplating killing himself. You see what I mean? Those wonderful blissful times when he and I sat talking, those intimate moments we shared—well, now I know *those times didn't exist.* I felt connected, I shared everything, but it was a one-man show. He wasn't there. He wasn't blissful. He was thinking of offing himself. I don't know what's real anymore. I've fabricated my reality."

"How about *this* reality? This room? You and me? The way we are together?"

"I don't know what to trust, who to trust. There's no such thing as a 'we.' I'm truly alone. I doubt very much that you and I are experiencing the same thing this very moment, right now as we speak."

"I want us to be a 'we' as much as possible. There's always an unbridgeable gap between two people, but I want to make that gap as small as possible here in this room."

"But Irv, I'm only *guessing* what you think and feel. And look how wrong I was about James. I guessed we were doing a duet, but it was a solo number. I've no doubt I'm doing the same here, guessing wrong about you." Charles hesitated and then suddenly asked, "What *are* you thinking right now?"

Twenty or thirty years ago such a question would have truly rattled me. But as I've matured as a therapist, I've grown to trust my unconscious to behave in a professionally responsible manner, and I know full well that it is not so much *what* I say about my thoughts that is important but rather *that I am willing to express them*. So I said the first thing that came into my mind.

"My thought at the moment you asked that question was very odd. It was something I saw recently posted on an anonymous website for secrets. It read, 'I work at Starbucks and when customers are rude I give them decaf.'"

Charles looked up at me, stunned, and then suddenly erupted into laughter. "What? What's that got to do with anything?"

"You asked what I was thinking, and *that's* what popped into my mind: *that everyone has secrets*. Let me try to track it. That train of thought started a couple of minutes earlier, when you spoke of the nature of reality and how you fabricate it. And then I started thinking of how right you are. Reality is not just something out there but something each of us constructs, or fabricates, to a significant degree. Then, for a moment—bear with me; you asked what I was thinking—I thought of the German philosopher, Kant, and how he taught us that the structure of our minds actively influences the nature of the reality we experience. And then I started thinking of all the deep secrets I've heard over my half century of practice as a therapist and reflecting that, however much we crave to merge with another, there will always remain distance. Then I started to think of how your experience of the color red or the taste of coffee and my experience of 'red' and 'coffee' will be very different in ways we can never really know. Coffee—*that's it; that's the link to the Starbucks secret.* But sorry, sorry Charles, I'm afraid I'm wandering far from where you may be."

"No, no, not at all."

"Tell me what passed through *your* mind as I spoke."

"I thought, 'Right on.' I like your speaking like this. I like your sharing your thoughts."

"Well, here's another one that just came up, an old memory of a case presentation at a seminar when I was a student, ages ago. The patient was a man who had a blissful honeymoon on some tropical island, one of the great times of his life. But the marriage deteriorated rapidly during the next year, and they divorced. He learned at some point from his wife that, throughout their time together, including their honeymoon, she had been obsessed with another man. His reaction was very similar to yours. He realized that their idyllic relationship on the tropical island was not a shared experience, that he, too, was playing a solo. I don't recall much more, but I do recall that he, like you, sensed that reality was fractured."

"Reality fractured . . . that speaks to me. It's even there in my dreams. Last night I had some powerful dreams but can only recall a bit. I was inside of a dolls' house and touched the curtains and windows and felt how they were paper and cellophane. It felt flimsy, and then I heard loud footsteps and was afraid that someone would stamp on the house."

"Charles, let me check in again about our reality right now. I give you notice: I'm going to keep doing this. How are you and I doing now?"

"Better than anywhere else, I guess. I mean we're more honest. But still there are some gaps. No, not *some* gaps—there are *big* gaps. We're not *really* sharing reality."

"Well, let's keep on trying to narrow the gaps. What questions do you have for me?"

"Hmm. You've never asked that before. Well, many questions. How do you see me? What's it like to be in the room with me right now? How hard is this hour for you?"

"Fair questions. I'll just let my thoughts run and not try to be systematic. I'm moved by what you're going through. I'm one hundred percent in this room. I like you, and I respect you—I think you know that—or I hope you do. And I have a strong desire to help you. I think of how you've been haunted by your father's death, how it's left its mark on your whole life. And I think of how awful it's been to have found something precious in your relationship with James Perry and then to have that wrenched away from you so suddenly. I imagine, also, that the loss of your father and of James looms large in your feelings toward me. Let's see what else comes to mind. I can tell you that when I meet with you, I face two different feelings that sometimes get in the way of one another. On the one hand, I want to be like a father to you, but I also want to help you get past the need for a father."

Charles nodded as I spoke, looked down, and remained silent. I asked, "And *now*, Charles, how real are we being?"

"I've misspoken. The truth is that the major problem isn't *you*. It's *me*. There's too much I've been withholding . . . too much I've been unwilling to say."

"For fear of driving me away?"

Charles shook his head. "Partly."

I was certain now I knew what it was: it was my age. I'd been through this with other patients. "For fear of giving me pain," I said.

He nodded.

"Trust me: it's my job to take care of my feelings. I'll hang in there with you. Try to make a start."

Charles loosened his necktie and unbuttoned his top button. "Well, here's one of last night's dreams. I was talking to you in your office, only it looked like a woodshop—I noticed a stack of wood and a large table saw, a plane, and a sander. Then suddenly you shrieked, grabbed your chest, and slumped forward. I jumped up to help you. I called 911 and held you till they came, and then I helped them put you on a stretcher. There was more, but that's all I can remember."

"Hunches about that dream?"

"Well, it's very transparent. I'm very conscious of your age and worried about your dying. The woodshop element is obvious, too. In the dream I've blended you with Mr. Reilly, my woodshop teacher in junior high school. He was very old, a bit of a father figure to me. In fact we all called him Pop Riley. Even after I graduated I used to visit him."

"And feelings in the dream?"

"It's vague, but I recall panic and also a lot of pride in my helping you."

"It's good you're bringing this up. Can you speak of other dreams that you've avoided telling me?"

"Uh, well. It's uncomfortable, but there was one a week or ten days ago that stuck in my mind. In the dream we were meeting like we are now in these chairs, but there were no walls, and I couldn't tell if we were inside or outside. You were grim-faced, and you leaned toward me and told me you had only six months to live. And then . . . this is really weird . . . I tried to strike a bargain with you: I would teach you how to die, and you would teach me how to be a therapist. I don't remember much else except that we were both crying a lot."

"The first part is clear—of course you're aware of my age and worried about how long I'll live. But what about the second part, wanting to be a therapist?"

"I don't know what to make of that. I've never thought I could be a therapist. It would be beyond me. I don't think I could deal with facing strong feelings all the time, and I do know I admire you a great deal. You've been kind, very kind, to me and always know how to point me in just the right direction." Charles leaned over to take a Kleenex and wipe his brow.

"This is very difficult for me. You've given me so much, and here I sit inflicting pain by telling you these dreadful dreams about you. This is not right."

"Your job here is to share your thoughts with me, and you're doing it well. *Of course* my age concerns you. We both know that at my age, at eighty-one, I'm approaching the end of my life. You're now grieving for James and also for your father, and it's only natural that you're worried about losing me as well. Eighty-one is old, shockingly old. I'm shocked myself when I think about it. I don't feel old, and over and over I wonder how I got to be eighty-one. I always used to be the youngest kid—in my classes, on my summer camp baseball team, on the tennis team—and now suddenly I'm the oldest person anywhere I go—restaurants, movies, professional conferences. I can't get used to it."

I took a deep breath. We sat quietly for a few moments. "Before we go further, I want to stop for another check, Charles. How are we doing now? How about the size of the gap?"

"The gap has narrowed quite a lot. But this is really hard. This is not normal conversation. You don't usually say to someone, 'I'm worried about your dying.' This has got to be painful for you, and right now you're one of the last persons in the world I want to hurt."

"But this is an unusual place. Here, we have, or we *should* have, no taboos against honesty. And keep in mind you're not bringing up anything I haven't thought about a great deal. A central part of the ethos of this field is keeping your eyes open to everything."

Charles nodded. Another brief silence passed between us.

"We're having far more silences today than ever before," I ventured.

Charles nodded again. "I'm really all here and totally with you. It's just that this discussion is taking my breath away."

"There's something else important I want to tell you. Believe it or not, looking at the end of life has some positive effects. I want to tell you of an odd experience I had a few days ago. It was about six o'clock, and I saw my wife at the end of our driveway reaching into our mailbox. I walked toward her. She turned her head and smiled. Suddenly and inexplicably, my mind shifted the scene, and for just a few moments I imagined being in a dark room watching a flickering home movie of scenes from my life. I felt much like the protagonist in *Krapp's Last Tape*. You know that Samuel Beckett play?"

"No, but I've heard of it."

"It's a monologue given by an old man on his birthday as he listens to tape recordings he has made on past birthdays. So, somewhat like Krapp, I imagined a film of old scenes of my life. And there I saw my dead wife turning toward me with a large smile, beckoning to me. As I watched her, I was flooded with poignancy and unimaginable grief. Then suddenly it all vanished, and I snapped back to the present, and there she was, alive, radiant, in the flesh, flashing her beautiful September smile. A warm flush of joy washed over me. I felt grateful that she and I were still alive, and I rushed to embrace her and to begin our evening walk."

I couldn't describe that experience without tears welling up, and I reached for a Kleenex. Charles also took a Kleenex to dab his eyes, "So you're saying, 'Count your blessings.'"

"Yes, exactly. I'm saying that anticipating endings may encourage us to grasp the present with greater vitality."

Charles and I both glanced at the clock. We had run over a few minutes. He slowly gathered his things. "I'm wiped out," he whispered. "You've got to be tired too."

I stood up straight, shoulders squared. "Not at all. Actually, a deep and true session like this one enlivens me. You worked hard today, Charles. We worked hard together."

I opened the office door for him, and, as always, we shook hands as he left. I closed the door and then suddenly slapped myself on the forehead and said, "No, I can't do this. I can't end the session this way." So I opened the door, called him back, and said, "Charles, I just slipped back into an old mode and did exactly what I don't want to do. The truth is I *am* tired from that hard deep work, a bit wiped out in fact, and I'm grateful I have no one else on my schedule today." I looked at him and waited. I didn't know what to expect.

"Oh Irv, I knew that. I know you better than you think I do. I know when you're just trying to be therapeutic."

~ 3 ~

Arabesque

I was perplexed. After fifty years in practice I thought I had seen everything, but I had never before had a new patient enter my office offering me a photograph of herself in the bloom of youth. And I was even more unnerved when this patient, Natasha, a portly Russian woman of seventy or so, stared as intently at me as I stared at the photograph of a beautiful ballerina in arabesque pose, balanced majestically on one toe and stretching both arms gracefully upward. I turned my glance back to Natasha, who, though no longer slender, had coasted to her seat with a dancer's grace. She must have sensed I was trying to locate the young dancer in her, for she raised her chin and turned her head just a bit to offer me a clear profile. Natasha's facial features had been coarsened, perhaps by too many Russian winters and too much alcohol. Still, she was an attractive woman, though not as beautiful as before, I thought, as I glanced once again at the photograph of the young Natasha, a marvel of elegance.

"Was I not lovely?" she coyly asked. When I nodded, she continued. "I was a prima ballerina at La Scala."

"Do you always think of yourself in the past tense?"

She drew herself back. "What a rude question, Dr. Yalom. Obviously you've taken the bad manners course that is required for all therapists. But," she paused to consider the matter, "perhaps it is so. Perhaps you are right. But what is strange in the case of Natalya the ballerina is that I was finished as a dancer before I was thirty—forty years ago—and I've been happier, ever so much happier, since I stopped dancing."

"You stopped dancing forty years ago and yet here, today, you enter my office offering me this picture of you as a young dancer. Surely you must feel that I would be uninterested in the Natasha of today?"

She blinked two or three times and then looked about for a minute, inspecting the décor of my office. "I had a dream about you last night," she said. "If I close my eyes, I can still see it. I was coming to see you and entered a room. It wasn't like this office. Perhaps it was your home, and there were a lot of people there, perhaps your wife and family, and I was carrying a big canvas bag full of rifles and cleaning equipment for them. I could see you surrounded by people in one corner, and I knew it was you from the picture on the cover of your Schopenhauer novel. I couldn't make my way to you or even catch your eye. There was more, but that's all I recall."

"Ah, and do you see any link between your dream and your offering me this photograph?"

"Rifles mean penises. I know that from a long psychoanalysis. My analyst told me I used the penis as a weapon. When I had an argument with my boyfriend, Sergei, the lead dancer in the company and, later, my husband, I would go out, get drunk, find a penis, any penis—the particular owner was incidental—and have sex in order to wound Sergei and make me feel better. It always worked. But briefly. Very briefly."

"And the link between the dream and the photograph?"

"The same question? You persist? Perhaps you're insinuating that I am using this picture of my young self to interest you in me sexually? Not only is this insulting, but it makes no sense whatsoever."

Her grand entrance holding the photograph was loaded with meaning. Of that I had no doubt, but I let it go for the moment and got down to business in a more direct fashion. "Please, let's now consider your reasons for contacting me. From your email I know you will be in San Francisco for only a short time and that it was extraordinarily urgent I meet with you today and tomorrow because you felt you were 'lost outside of your life and couldn't find your way back.' Please tell me about that. You wrote that it was a matter of life and death."

"Yes, that's what it feels like. It's very hard to describe, but something serious is happening to me. I've come to visit California with my husband, Pavel, and we've done what we've always done on such visits. He met with some important clients; we've seen our Russian friends, driven to Napa Valley, gone to the San Francisco opera, and dined at fine restaurants. But somehow this time it's not the same. How to put it? The Russian word is *ostrannaya*. I'm not truly here. Nothing that happens sinks in. I have insulation around me; I feel it is not *me* here, not me experiencing these things. I'm anxious, very distracted. And not sleeping well. I wish my English was better to describe things. Once I lived in the US for four years and took many lessons, but my English still feels clumsy."

"Your English so far is excellent, and you're doing a good job describing how you feel. Tell me, how do you explain it? What do *you* think is happening to you?"

"I'm bewildered. I mentioned I needed a four-year psycho-analysis long ago, when I was in terrible crisis. But even then I did not have *this* feeling. And since then life has been good. Until now I've been completely well for many years."

"This state of not being in your life. Let's try to trace it back. When do you think this feeling began? How long ago?"

"I can't say. It's such an odd feeling and a vague feeling that it's hard to pinpoint it. I know we've been in California for about three days."

"Your email to me was written a week ago; that was before you came to California. Where were you at that time?"

"We spent a week in New York, then a few days in Washington, and then flew here."

"Anything unsettling happen in New York or Washington?"

"Nothing. Just the usual jet lag. Pavel had several business meetings, and I was alone to explore. Usually I love exploring cities."

"And this time? Tell me exactly what you did while he was working."

"In New York, I walked. I . . . how do you say it in English? . . . looked at people? People watched?"

"Yes, people watched."

"So I people watched, and I shopped and spent days visiting the Met museum. Oh yes, I am certain I felt good in New York because I remember that, on one beautiful sunny day, Pavel and I took a boat trip excursion around Ellis Island and the Statue of Liberty, and I remember we both felt so wonderful. So it was *after* New York that I started going downhill."

"Try to recall the trip to Washington. What did you do?"

"I did what I always do. I followed my usual pattern. I visited Smithsonian museums every day: the Air and Space, Natural History, American History, and, oh yes, yes! There *was* one strong event when I visited the National Gallery."

"What happened? Try to describe it."

"I was so excited when I saw a huge outside banner announcing an exhibition on the history of ballet."

"Yes, and what happened?"

"As soon as I saw that banner, I rushed inside the gallery, so excited that I pushed and forced my way to the front of the line. I was looking for something. I believe I was looking for Sergei."

"Sergei? You mean your first husband?"

"Yes, my first husband. This won't really make sense to you unless I tell you some things about my life. May I present some of my highlights? I've been rehearsing a speech for days."

Concerned that she was about to go on stage and that her presentation might use up all our time, I responded, "Yes, a brief summary would be helpful."

"To start, you must know I absolutely lacked mothering and my lifelong feeling of lack of mothering was the central focus of my analysis. I was born in Odessa, and my parents separated before I was born. I never knew my father, and my mother never spoke of him. My mother hardly spoke of anything. Poor woman, she was always ill and died from cancer just before I was ten. I remember at my tenth birthday party . . . "

"Natasha, sorry to interrupt, but I have a dilemma. Believe me, I'm interested in all you have to say, but at the same time, I've got to be timekeeper here because we have only these two sessions, and I want, for your sake, to use our time efficiently."

"You're absolutely right. When I'm on stage, I forget the time. I'll rush now and promise you to take no side excursions. At any rate, after my mother died, her twin sister, Aunt Olga, took me to St. Petersburg and raised me. Now Aunt Olga was a kind person, and she was always good to me, but she had to support herself—she was unmarried—and she worked hard and had little time for me. She was a very good violinist and traveled with the symphony orchestra much of the year. She knew I was a good dancer, and about a year after I arrived, she arranged for auditions, where I performed well enough for her to deposit me in the Vaganova Ballet Academy, where I spent the next eight years. I became such a good dancer that, at the age of eighteen, I received an offer from the Kirov Opera and Ballet Theater, where I danced for a few years. That was where I met Sergei, one of the great dancers and egotists and philanderers of our time and who is also the great love of my life."

"You use the present tense? Still the great love of your life?"

Bristling a bit at my interruption, she said, sharply, "Please let me continue. You asked me to rush, and I'm hurrying, and I want to relate this in my own way. Sergei and I married, and, almost miraculously, he and I managed to defect when he accepted an offer with La Scala in Italy. After all, tell me, who could live in Russia in those years? Now I must discuss Sergei—he had a leading role in my life. Less than a year after we married, I was crippled with pain, and the doctor told me I had gout. Tell me, can you imagine a more catastrophic illness for a ballerina? No, there is none! Gout ended my career before I was thirty. And, then, what did Sergei, the love of my life, do? He immediately left me for another dancer. And what did I do? I went quite crazy and almost killed myself with alcohol and almost killed him with a broken bottle and I slashed scars on his face to remember me by. My aunt Olga had to come to take me from the Milan psychiatric hospital and bring me back to Russia, and *that's* when I started the psychoanalysis that saved my life. My aunt found one of the only psychoanalysts in all of Russia, and even he was practicing underground. Much of my analysis was about Sergei, about getting over the pain he gave me, about quitting alcohol forever, about ending my parade of shallow affairs. And maybe about learning how to love—love myself and love others.

"When I improved, I attended the university, and in music studies I soon found out, to my surprise, that I had talent for the cello, not enough to perform but enough to teach, and I have been a cello teacher ever since. Pavel, my husband, was one of my first students. The worst cellist I ever saw, but a wonderful man and, as it turned out later, a very smart and successful businessman. We fell in love, he divorced his wife for me, and we married and have had a long, marvelous life together."

"Very succinct and wonderfully clear, Natasha. Thank you."

"As I say, I've been rehearsing it in my mind many times. You see why I didn't want any interruptions?"

"Yes, I understand. So now let's return to the museum in Washington. By the way, if there are words I use you don't understand, please stop me and tell me."

"So far I understand everything. My vocabulary is good, and I read many American novels to keep up my English. Right now I read *Henderson the Rain King.*"

"You have good taste. That is one of my favorite books, and Bellow is one of our great writers, though he is no Dostoevsky. But to return to the exhibit, after what you've told me, I can appreciate how emotional it must have been for you. Tell me exactly what happened. You said you entered looking for Sergei, the man you said 'is the love of your life'?"

"Yes, I'm quite sure now that Sergei was my agenda, my secret agenda when I entered the exhibition. And I mean secret even from myself. The love of my life doesn't necessarily mean my *conscious* life. You, a famous psychiatrist, should appreciate that."

"Mea culpa." I found her soft jabs rather charming and enlivening.

"I forgive you—just this once. Now to my visit to the exhibit. They showed a lot of early Russian posters from the Bolshoi and the Kirov, and one of them, hanging near the entrance, was a stunning picture of Sergei flying like an angel through the air in Swan Lake. It was somewhat blurred, but I'm sure it was Sergei, even though his name was not given. I searched for hours through the entire exhibition, but there was no mention of his name, not one single time. Can you believe it? Sergei was like a god, and yet his name no longer exists. Now I remember . . . "

"What? What do you remember?"

"You asked when I first began to lose myself. It happened *then*. I remember walking out of that exhibit as though I were in a trance, and I've not felt like myself since."

"Do you recall searching also for yourself in the museum? For pictures or mentions of *your* name?"

"I don't remember that day very well. So I have to rebuild it. Is that the right word?"

"I understand. You have to reconstruct it."

"Yes, I must reconstruct the visit. I think that I was so shocked by Sergei not being included that I said to myself, 'If he was not there, how could I possibly be included?' But perhaps in a timid way I did look for myself. There were some undated photos of La Scala's *Giselle*—for two seasons I played Myrtha— and I do remember peering so closely at one photo that my nose touched the photograph and the guard ran over, glowered at me, and pointed to an imaginary line on the floor and told me not to cross it."

"It seems such a human thing to do, to look for yourself in those historical photos."

"But what right did I have to look for myself? I repeat—I still don't think you've registered it. You're not listening. You've not grasped that Sergei was a god, that he soared above us in the clouds, and all of us, all the other dancers, gazed upon him as children upon a majestic airship."

"I'm puzzled. Let me summarize what I know so far about Sergei. He was a great dancer, and the two of you performed together in Russia, and then, when he defected to dance in Italy, you chose to go with him and then married him. And then when you got gout, he promptly abandoned you and took up with another woman, at which point you became extremely disturbed and slashed him with a broken bottle. Right so far?"

Natasha nodded, "Right."

"After you left Italy with your aunt, what further contact did you have with Sergei?"

"None. Nothing. I never saw him again. Never heard from him again. Not one word."

"But you kept thinking about him?"

"Yes, at first when I heard his name mentioned, I'd obsess about him and had to bang my head to knock him out of my brain. But, eventually, I blotted him from my memory. I cut him out."

"He did you great harm, and you cut him out of your memory, but last week you went into that National Gallery exhibit thinking of him as 'the love of your life,' searching for him, and then grew outraged that he had been overlooked and forgotten. You can see my confusion."

"Yes, yes, I understand you. A big contradiction, I agree. Going to that museum show was like performing an excavation in my mind. It's like I blindly struck a massive vein of energy that has now come spewing out. I speak in a clumsy way. Do you understand?"

When I nodded, Natasha continued, "Sergei was four years older than me, so he is now about seventy-three. That is, if he is alive. And yet I cannot imagine a seventy-three-year-old

Sergei. It's impossible. Believe me, if you knew him, you'd understand. In my mind I see only that young beautiful dancer in the poster sailing forever through the air. Have I heard from him? No, not one word from him since I slashed his face so long ago! I could find out. I could probably find him on the Internet, perhaps Facebook, but I'm afraid to search."

"Afraid of?"

"Almost everything. That he's dead. Or that he is still beautiful and wants me. That we'll email and that the pain in my breast will be unbearable and that I'll fall in love again. That I'll leave Pavel and go to Sergei wherever he is."

"You speak as though your life with Sergei is simply frozen in time and exists somewhere and that, if you revisit it, everything—the mutual love, the soaring passions, even the youthful beauty—will be exactly the same."

"So true."

"Whereas the truth, the real-life scenario, is that Sergei will either be dead or look like a seventy-three-year-old wrinkled man, most likely grey- or white-haired or bald, possibly a bit stooped, possibly feeling entirely differently from you about your time together, perhaps not thinking very kindly of you every time he looks at his scarred face in the mirror."

"Talk that talk all you want, but at this very moment I'm not listening to what you are saying. Not one word."

Time was up, and as she stepped toward the door, she noted her photograph on the table and started back for it. I picked it up and handed it to her. Putting it back into her purse, she said, "I'll see you tomorrow, but no more words about this picture. *Basta!*"

"I fly to Odessa tonight," she said as we began the following day, "and I slept so poorly because of you that I'm not very sad this is our last meeting. Your words about Sergei were cruel, you know. Very cruel. Please answer this question: Do you speak like that to all your patients?"

"Please consider it a compliment to the strength I see in you."

With a slightly quizzical expression she pursed her lips, started to answer, but then checked herself and instead took a long look at me. She exhaled and leaned back into her chair. Then she said, "All right, I hear you. I'm ready. Listening. Waiting."

"Please begin by telling me more about the thoughts that kept you awake last night."

"I slept only in short bursts because most of the night I was haunted by one dream which kept going on and on with one version after another. I am visiting the Congo with some delegation, and suddenly I can't find any of the others, and I am alone. I realize I may be in the most dangerous spot on earth, and I get panicky. Then, in one version, I am walking in a deserted neighborhood knocking on doors and finding them all bolted and no one around. In another version, I enter a deserted house and hide in a closet as I hear loud pounding footsteps approaching outside. Or, in another version, I use my cell phone to call my delegation, but I do not know my location, and so I cannot tell them where I am. I suggest they bring lanterns and wave them, so I can see them from the window. But then I realize I am in a huge city, and that is a hopeless suggestion.

"And so it went all night long, waiting in terror for some horror to find and to take me." She put her hand on her chest. "Even now my heart is pounding just telling you the dream."

"A nightmare continuing all night long. How terrible! What hunches do you have about the dream? Think about it, and tell me whatever comes to mind."

"I know I read something in the paper the other day about atrocities in Africa and the children's army killing all in their path, but I stopped myself from reading too much. I always have a bad night after reading something like that. If I see a killing on TV, I turn it off, and I can't count the many movies I've walked out of for the same reason."

"Keep going. Tell me all you remember of that dream."

"That's all. I'm in a spot where, over and over, my life is in danger."

"Think of that statement, 'My life is in danger.' Just free-associate to it, by which I mean: you try to let your mind run free and just observe it as though from a distance and describe all the thoughts that run across it, almost as though you were watching a screen."

After exhaling and flashing a look of exasperation, Natasha leaned her head against the back of her chair and whispered, "My life is in danger, my life is in danger," and then grew silent.

After a minute or two, I prodded her, "A little louder, please."

"I know what *you* want to hear."

"And you don't want to say it to me."

She nodded.

"Try imagining this," I continued. "You continue to be silent here today until our time is up. Imagine you are leaving my office. How *then* would you feel?"

"All right! I'll say it! *Of course* my life is in danger! I'm sixty-nine years old. How much life do I have ahead? My life was all back there. My real life!"

"Your real life? You mean on the stage, dancing with Sergei?"

"Did *you* ever dance?"

"Only tap dancing. I used to imitate all the Fred Astaire routines, sometimes at home, sometimes outside on the street."

Natasha's eyes popped open, and she stared at me in astonishment.

"I'm joking. I'm one of the world's worst dancers, but I'm an avid watcher, and I can imagine how glorious it was for you to perform before those large applauding audiences."

"You're quite playful for a psychiatrist, you know. And a bit seductive."

"How is that for you?"

"Just right."

"Good. Then teach me about the real life back then."

"Life was so exhilarating. The crowds, the photographers, the heavenly music, the costumes, and Sergei—believe me, one of the most beautiful men in the world—and the alcohol and the intoxication of the dance and, yes, the wild sex. Everything that has followed pales in comparison." Natasha, who had been sitting on the edge of her chair as she spoke, now relaxed and leaned back.

"Where do your thoughts go now?"

"Here's something I should tell you: lately I've been having a strange thought, that every day I live now, even a very good day, is also a day of sorrow because it takes me further and further from my real life. Is that not odd?"

"It's as I said earlier. It's as though that real life still exists in suspended animation. And if we had the right transportation, we could go to it, and you could show me around and point out all the familiar things. You know what I mean?"

When Natasha nodded, I went on. "And in a way that idea is the key to understanding your trip to the museum. You weren't just looking for Sergei; you were looking for your lost life, even though the adult part of your mind knows that everything is transient, that the past exists only in the mind and your early world is now only a memory, an electric or chemical signal stored somewhere in your brain.

"Natasha," I continued, "I understand your situation in life. I'm a lot older than you, and I am dealing with the same issues. For me one of the darkest things about death is that when I die, my whole world—that is, my world of memories, that rich world peopled by everyone I've ever known, that world that seems so rooted in granite—will vanish with me. Poof! Just like that. The last couple of weeks I've been cleaning out boxes of old papers and photos, and I look at them, perhaps a picture of some street in my childhood neighborhood or some friend or relative whom no one else alive ever knew, and I throw them away, and each time I do, something shudders inside as I see pieces of my old real world flaking away."

Natasha drew a deep breath and in a softer voice said, "I understand everything you say. Thank you for telling me that. It means a lot when you speak personally like this. I know you speak the truth, but it is hard to absorb such truth. I tell you something: right now, at this very moment, I feel Sergei vibrating in my mind. I know he struggles to stay there, to stay in existence, dancing forever."

"I want to say something more about Sergei," I told her. "I know a lot of people who have gone back to high school reunions and immediately fell in love, sometimes with an old boyfriend, often with someone they did not know well. Many settled into a late-life marriage, some successful, but some disastrous. I believed many of them loved via association, that is they loved youthful joyousness, their early school days, and their dreamy anticipations of an exciting life, stretching out magically and immeasurably before them. But it wasn't falling in love with someone in particular. It was making that person a symbol of all that joyousness of their youths. What I'm trying to say is that Sergei was part of that magical time of youth, and because he was there at that time you imbued him with love— that is, *you put the love into him*."

Natasha remained silent. After a couple of minutes I asked, "What's passing through your mind during this silence?"

"I was thinking about your book title, *Love's Executioner*."

"And you feel I'm being love's executioner with you?"

"You cannot deny that?"

"Keep in mind that you told me you fell in love with Pavel and have had a marvelous life with him, and when you said that, I felt nothing but pleasure about you and him. So it's not love I'm stalking. My prey is the mirage of love."

Silence.

"A little louder."

"I hear such a soft voice, a whisper, inside."

"And it says? . . ."

"It says, 'Damn you, I'm not giving Sergei up.'"

"It requires time, and you have to go about this at your own pace. Let me ask you a different question: I wonder if you've experienced any change since we started?"

"Change? What do you mean?"

"Yesterday you described that awful dizzying feeling of being outside of life, of not experiencing anything, of not being present. Is that symptom any different now? It seems to me you are very much here in our sessions."

"I can't deny that—you are right. I cannot be more 'here' than right now. Holding my feet in boiling oil does powerfully concentrate my mind."

"You think me cruel?"

"Cruel? Not exactly cruel, but tough, real tough."

I glanced at the clock. Only a few minutes remained. How to use them most effectively?

"I wonder, Natasha, if you have questions you want to ask me?"

"Hmm, that's unusual. Yes, I have a question. How do *you* do it? How do you cope with being eighty and feeling the end approaching closer and closer?"

As I thought about my reply, she said, "No, I'm the cruel one. Forgive me, I shouldn't have asked that."

"There's nothing cruel in your question. I like your asking it. I'm trying to formulate, to put together, an honest answer. There's a Schopenhauer quote that compares love passion with the blinding sun. When it dims in later years, we suddenly become aware of the wondrous starry heavens that had been obscured, or hidden, by the sun. So for me the vanishing of youthful, sometimes tyrannical, passions has made me appreciate the starry skies more and all wonders of being alive, wonders that I had previously overlooked. I'm in my eighties, and I'll tell you something unbelievable: I've never felt better or more at peace with myself. Yes, I know my existence is drawing to a close, but the end has been there since the beginning. What is different now is that I treasure the pleasures of sheer awareness, and I'm fortunate enough to share them with my wife, whom I've known almost all of my life."

"Thank you. Once again, I tell you how important it is when you speak personally to me. It's funny, but just as you were speaking, a dream that I had earlier this week sprang into my mind. I had forgotten it, but it's just come back, and it's very clear now. I was walking on a deserted road, and somehow I knew that the last one who used this road was my dog, Baloo. Then I saw Baloo by the side of the road and went to him, leaned over, and looked right into his eyes. And I thought, *You and I are both living souls*, and then I thought, *I'm no better than him.*"

"And the feelings that accompany this dream?"

"At first I was so glad to see my dog again. You see, Baloo died three weeks before we left for the US. He was my companion for sixteen years, and I've had a hard time getting over my sadness. In fact I welcomed my trip to the US because I thought it might help me get over my grief. Are you a dog owner? If not, you won't understand."

"No, I'm a cat lover, though, and I think I can appreciate the depth of your pain."

She hesitated and nodded as though she were satisfied with my answer. "Yes, it was very deep. My husband says too deep. He thinks I was over-attached to Baloo and that he was a substitute child. I don't think I told you that I have no children."

"So, in the dream, you're traveling on the same road that Baloo took weeks before, and then you looked deep into his eyes and said, 'We're both living souls, and I'm no better than you.' What do you think the dream is trying to communicate?"

"I know what *you'd* think."

"Tell me."

"That I know I'm walking on the road to death like Baloo."

"Like all living souls."

"Yes, like all living souls."

"And you, what do *you* think?"

"I think this whole conversation is making things worse for me."

"In that you're more uncomfortable."

"A few more healing sessions like this, and I'll need to go home by ambulance."

"All the symptoms you described yesterday—being removed from life, being insulated, not being in your life—all served to anesthetize yourself from the pain inherent in being a living soul. Let's look at how we began. You entered my office with your photograph—"

"Oh no, not that again!"

"I know you forbade me to discuss it, but I'm disobeying you because it's too important. Please listen to what I'm going to say. You know all this already. I'm not telling you anything you don't already know. It's just easier to fend off something told to you from the outside than it is something rising from the depths of yourself. I believe that some part of you had already arrived at the same conclusion I'm suggesting to you. It's all there in that dream about traveling the same road as Baloo. I'm struck that your dream, which offers the key to our puzzle, returned to you just as we prepared to stop. And the photograph you gave me at the beginning was a hint to me about what direction I should take with you."

"You say I knew all this? You give me far, far too much credit."

"I don't think so. I'm just siding with the part of you where wisdom dwells."

We both looked at the clock. We had run over several minutes. As Natasha rose and collected her things, she said, "May I get back to you by email or Skype if I have more questions?"

"Of course. But remember: I'm aging. So don't wait too long."

~ 4 ~

Thank You, Molly

A few months ago I attended an outdoor funeral service for Molly, my long-term bookkeeper and Jane-of-all-trades who had worked for me for decades and had been both a godsend and a major thorn in my side. I'd first employed her in 1980 to collect my mail and pay my bills while I was on a year's sabbatical, living and writing in Asia and Europe. When I returned, Molly soon grew dissatisfied with her bit role and little by little began to insinuate herself into all my domestic matters. Soon she was managing all our financial and household affairs, paying bills, taking care of correspondence, and filing papers, manuscripts, and contracts. She discharged my gardener and installed her own gardening team and, later, her own team of painters, and cleaners, and handymen—though, if the job were small, she insisted on doing it herself.

There was no stopping her. One day I came home to find several trucks in our driveway and Molly at the base of a huge oak, calling to a man a hundred feet above, telling him which branches to saw off. I was surprised that she was not up in the tree herself. She insisted that she had discussed this project with me, but I was certain she had not. That was the final straw, and I fired her on the spot and fired her again on at least three other occasions, but she would have none of it. Whenever I objected to her fees, she reminded me, quite correctly, of the many tortured evenings my wife and I had spent paying bills and balancing our checkbooks until she had come along, and then suggested I work two more hours each month to pay her salary. She insisted she was indispensable, and my firings and objections were never issued wholeheartedly because I knew she was right. I was greatly grieved at her death from pancreatic cancer, and I knew I was never to find her replacement.

Molly's funeral was held on a glorious sunny afternoon in her son's large backyard. I was surprised to see several Stanford colleagues there. I'd had no idea they'd been her clients too, but I recalled she honored a rigorous confidentiality code, steadfastly refusing to reveal the identities of any of her customers. At the end of the memorial service, I immediately rose to leave in order to pick up some friends at the airport, but just as I opened the gate to the street, I heard my name called and turned to see a stately older man wearing a stunning broad-brimmed panama hat approaching me, escorted by an exceedingly lovely woman. Seeing that I did not immediately recognize him, he introduced himself, "I'm Alvin Cross, and this is my wife, Monica. I saw you for therapy half a lifetime ago."

I hate these awkward situations. Facial recognition has never been my strong suit, and as I've aged, it has progressively deteriorated. At the same time I felt it would be hurtful for this former patient to learn I didn't remember him, so I stalled for time, waiting and hoping for memories of him to coast into my mind. "Alvin, good to see you. And good to meet you, Monica."

"Irv Yalom," she said, "it's such a pleasure to meet you. I've heard so much about you from Al. I think I owe our meeting and our marriage and our two wonderful children to you."

"That is quite wonderful to hear. Sorry to be so slow on recall, Alvin, but in a few minutes I'll remember everything about our time together—that's how it works at my age."

"I was then, still am, a radiologist at Stanford and came to see you shortly after my brother died," said Alvin, trying to stimulate my memory.

"Ah, yes, yes," I lied, "it's coming back to me. I'd really love a long talk and update on your post-therapy life, but I'm rushing to pick up friends at the airport. Could we meet for coffee and have a chat later this week?"

"Love to."

"You still at Stanford?"

"Yes." He took his card from his wallet and handed it to me.

"Thanks, I'll phone you tomorrow," I said, as I rushed off, mortified at my memory lapse.

Later that evening I went to my storage room to find my notes on Alvin. As I rifled through my files of patient records, I thought of all the deep, often uplifting, sometimes tragic, stories found in these records. Each one brought to mind the compelling two-person drama I had engaged in, and it was hard to tear myself away from reliving these old forgotten encounters.

I found Alvin Cross's file in my 1982 section, and though I saw him for only twelve hours, it was a thick file. In those precomputer days I had the luxury of a personal secretary, and I dictated long detailed notes of each session. I opened Alvin's file and started to read. Within a few minutes, presto: everything rematerialized in my mind.

Alvin Cross, a radiologist at Stanford Hospital, phoned and requested a consultation for some personal problems. Many Stanford doctors whom I see for therapy make a point of coming very punctually or even a couple of minutes late, entering my office at the Stanford Hospital furtively because they are queasy about being seen visiting a psychiatrist. But not Dr. Cross, who sat leisurely reading a magazine in the clinic waiting room. When I approached and introduced myself, he shook my hand with a firm grip, strode into my office in a calm and confident manner, and sat tall in his chair.

I began as I usually do in first sessions, by sharing whatever information I have. "All I know about you, Dr. Cross, comes from our phone conversation. You're a physician at Stanford Hospital, you heard my recent presentation at medical grand rounds about my psychotherapy work with patients dying from breast cancer, and you thought I might be able to be of help."

"Yes, that's right. You gave a refreshing and unusual talk. I've attended grand rounds for years, and this is the first one I've heard about human feelings and with no slides, data, or pathology reports."

My first impression of Alvin Cross was of a dignified, attractive man in his thirties, with angular features, slight graying at his temples, and a self-assured way of speaking. He and I were dressed the same, each wearing white hospital coats with our names sewed in dark blue cursive letters on our left upper pocket.

"So tell me, what did I say at grand rounds that made you think I could be of help?"

"It seemed you had tender feelings for your patients," he began. "And I was jolted by your description of an oncologist dispassionately giving your patient the results of her radiological scans. Of her terror at learning that her cancer had metastasized and her clinging tightly to her husband—her terror at being given a death sentence."

"Yes, I remember. But tell me the relevance of that for you and me today."

"Well, I'm the guy who writes those death sentences. I've been writing those kind of reports for a long time, for five years, yet your talk brought the job home to me in a different way."

"Made it more personal?"

"Exactly. In our radiology viewing rooms, we don't encounter the whole patient. We look for areas of calcifications or increased sizes of nodes. We look for oddities that we can show students—organs displaced by masses, decalcified bone in myeloma, distended bowel, an extra spleen. It's always about parts, body parts. It's never about whole people in whole bodies. But now I think about how patients feel and how their faces will look when doctors read them my x-ray reports, and I get a bit shaken up."

"Is this a recent change? Since my talk?"

"Oh, yes, very recent and, in part, due to your talk. Otherwise I couldn't have functioned in my work all these years. I know you wouldn't want your x-rays read by someone who is freaking out about how you're going to feel about his report."

"For sure. Our fields are so different, aren't they? I strive to be close; you strive to stay distant." He nodded, and I continued, "But you said, your changes were 'in part' due to my talk. Any hunch about what else was responsible?"

"More than a hunch. It was my brother's death a couple months ago. A few weeks before he died, he asked me to look at his films. Lung cancer. Heavy smoker."

"Tell me about you and your brother." As a psychiatric resident, I'd been taught to conduct a highly systematic interview starting with the presenting complaint and then following a protocol—a history of the present illness followed by an exploration of the patient's family, education, social life, sexual development, and vocational history—and then moving on to the intricacies of the psychiatric examination. But I had no intention of following any schema; it had been decades since I proceeded so systematically. Like all seasoned therapists, I work far more intuitively in my pursuit of information. I've come to trust my intuition so much I suspect I'm no longer a good teacher for neophytes, who require methodical guidelines in their early years.

"When my brother, Jason, called to ask me to consult on his films," Dr. Cross said, "it was the first time I had heard his voice in over fifteen years. We had had a falling out." He sighed and looked up at me, his lips quivering. I was surprised to see that. It was my first glimpse of vulnerability.

"Tell me about it," I spoke more gently now.

"Jason is two years younger—*was* two years younger—and I guess I was a tough act to follow. I was the good kid, always at the top of the class. Without fail, every time poor Jason entered a new school, he'd be greeted by a chorus of teachers talking about me and saying they hoped he would be the student that I was. Ultimately he chose not to compete, to opt out. In high school he rarely cracked a book and got heavily into drugs. Maybe he *couldn't* compete. I don't think he was all that bright.

"At the end of his senior year, he became involved with a girl who ended up defining his future. She was a fellow druggie, good-looking in a cheap way but intellectually limited: her life aspiration was to be a manicurist. They soon got engaged, and one evening he brought her home for dinner. That was a disaster of biblical proportion. I can still see the scene: the two of them, unwashed and unkempt, smooching the whole time, just flaunting it in everyone's face. My parents and grandparents were shocked and disgusted. Frankly, I was too.

"Everyone in the family detested his girlfriend, but no one said anything because they knew Jason would do the exact opposite. So my parents gave me the job of warning him about her. They also made me promise I wouldn't mention their having asked me to intervene. I had a big-brother talk with Jason and laid it all out. I told him that marriage was a momentous decision, that the time would come when he'd want more—a lot more—in a wife, that she'd drag him down. The next morning we woke up to find he had gone, along with all the money and silver in the house. He never spoke to any of us again."

"The family put you on the spot. Talk about a damned-if-you-do and damned-if-you-don't situation. Are there other siblings?"

"No, just the two of us. In retrospect, I think that maybe I could've been a better big brother and I should have tried harder to contact Jason years ago."

"Let's tag that and come back to it. First, tell me what happened to your brother after he split."

"He simply vanished. From that time on, all we ever had were a few stray scraps of information that drifted in from his acquaintances. He was doing construction work, then stone masonry. I heard he got reasonably good at it and ended up building fireplaces and stone walls. Continued heavy drug use. And then out of the blue, a couple of months ago, came the phone call. 'Alvin, this is Jason. I've got lung cancer. Would you look at my x-rays? My doctor said it would be OK for you to see them.'

"Of course, I agreed and got his doctor's name and promised to contact him that very day. I found out Jason was living in North Carolina, and I asked if I could visit him. After a pause, a pause long enough that I thought he'd hung up, he agreed."

I looked at Dr. Cross's face. He looked so taut and so sad that I wondered if this was too much, too soon. We'd hardly said hello before we had plunged into deep and very dark water. I gave him a breathing spell by reflecting on what had happened up to that point between us.

"My plan, as I told you on the phone, is that we meet today in consultation and see if starting therapy might be a good idea. Have you been in therapy before?"

He shook his head. "No, I'm a therapy virgin."

"Well, tell me, Dr. Cross—"

"If you don't mind, I'm fine with Alvin."

"Okay. And I'm Irv. So tell me, Alvin, what's it been like so far talking to me? Seems we've moved quickly into some heavy feelings. Perhaps too quickly?"

He shook his head. "Not at all."

"Are we on track? Is this what you hoped to discuss?"

"My reaction to Jason's death is exactly what I wanted to discuss. I'm just surprised—pleasantly surprised—that we're there already."

"Any questions for me so far?" I asked, wanting to establish the norm of free interchange.

He seemed puzzled, then shook his head, and said, "No. Most of all what I want to do is to tell you this story. I need to get this out in the open."

"Please, go on."

"So after Jason's call, I hopped on a plane to North Carolina and went to see him. In Raleigh I first stopped at his doctor's office and reviewed the films. Jason's tumor was deadly. It had infiltrated his left lung and metastasized to his ribs, spine, and brain. There was no hope.

"I drove an hour on the highway and then three miles down a North Carolina dirt road to a run-down house, little more than a shack really, although it contained an impressive stone fireplace he'd built for himself. I was shocked by his appearance. His cancer had already done much of its work and turned my younger brother into an old man. Jason was emaciated. His body was stooped, and his face was pallid and weary. And he smoked marijuana without stop. When I complained the fumes were getting to me, he switched to tobacco. 'Not a good idea with lung cancer,' I almost said, but held my tongue. Having looked at the films, I knew my words would be pointless. So there I sat, watching my cancer-riddled kid brother chain-smoke. I caught his glance a couple of times as he lit up. I'm certain I saw a look of defiance. I'll never forget that scene."

"Reminds me a bit of that dilemma you faced years before when you so disapproved of his choice of a mate. Damned if you spoke, damned if you didn't."

"I had the same thought. Continuing to smoke was crazy, but it would have been crazy for me to tell him so. And, for sure, telling him what I thought about his fiancée was the wrong choice back then, even though my prediction about the relationship proved accurate. I'm ashamed to say it, but I had a flash of satisfaction when he told me his wife had disappeared a few years earlier with their young daughter and all the money they had hidden in the house. He hadn't heard from her since. I have a hunch they'd been growing and peddling grass."

"So what happened next between the two of you?"

"I had one last shot at being a good big brother. I did my best. I asked what he'd been told about his condition. His doc had been straight with him—told him that treatment could do little and that statistics indicated he might expect only a few months of life. With a heavy heart, I confirmed the doc-tor's diagnosis and bleak prognosis. I offered some medical ad-vice about his pain management. I told him he wasn't alone, that I'd be there for him. I wanted to hug him, but the time gap was too wide to bridge. I offered money but was uneasy about it since he'd just use it for drugs. Still, I left him three hundred dollars on the kitchen table before I left. Perhaps he appreciated it, but he never acknowledged it. I didn't know what else I could do. He wouldn't consider coming to California, an offer I made only halfheartedly. Nor would he consider chemo or any other treatment that might have slowed the cancer a bit or made him more comfortable. 'It won't make any difference, and I don't give a shit,' he said. I tried my best to talk about our family and our past life together, but he said he wanted to forget all that. Perhaps, Irv, you might have known what else to say. I just hit a dead end. When I left, we agreed to stay in touch, but he had no phone. He said he'd use a neighbor's phone to call me."

"Did he?"

"Never did. And I couldn't reach him. Heard from a North Carolina hospital a few weeks ago that he died. I went back East to bury him in our family plot."

"What was that like for you?"

"Lonely. Only an elderly aunt and uncle were there, and a couple of cousins who barely knew him. My parents were killed ten years ago in a head-on car crash. At Jason's funeral, I kept thinking, over and over, that it was better my folks were dead and didn't have to see this. What a sad, wasted life."

"And it was then that your feelings changed about your work?"

"Yes, pretty soon after that. I just felt dread about going to work and viewing the films and writing reports informing patients they're going to die. Everything at work, especially chest films, reminded me of Jason."

I turned inward for a moment. It seemed pretty straightforward. A well-functioning man is traumatized by his brother's death, flooded with death anxiety, and traumatized repeatedly by reminders of death in his everyday work. I was pretty sure I understood what was going on and knew exactly how to help him. As our hour drew to a close, I told him that I thought I could help and suggested we meet weekly. He seemed relieved, as though he had just passed an audition.

The following session I obtained some background information. His father had been a family doctor in a rural Virginia area, and his mother worked by his side as a nurse in their home office. Alvin had taken a straight premed path at the University of Virginia and then went to medical school in New York and radiology residency in California. He was single; he'd had many relationships with women but none of any duration. Moreover, he had not been out with a woman since Jason's phone call.

I asked him for a detailed history of a recent, typical twenty-four-hour period, starting at bedtime. The exercise proved particularly illuminating with Alvin because I learned how little intimacy his life contained. Though he was busily involved with students and colleagues during his working day, he had little other human contact. He spent weekends alone, generally kayaking, and almost all of his meals were solitary affairs: breakfast and lunch at the hospital cafeteria and take-out food for dinners at home or a fast meal at some restaurant with counter seating, generally a sushi or oyster bar. His colleagues had long ago given up trying to fix him up with women and had come to view him as a committed bachelor. Some faculty wives had tried to turn him into a family uncle by inviting him for holiday or celebratory family dinners. He had no close male friends or confidants, and although he had a steady stream of dates—most (in that pre-Internet time) stemming from newspaper personal ads—the relationships always fizzled out after a date or two. Naturally, I inquired into the quick endings, but he never gave me a clear answer, and even more odd, he appeared curiously uncurious about the matter. I tagged that also for future exploration.

His sleep was generally good, usually seven to eight hours per night. Though he rarely remembered dreams, he recalled a recurrent nightmare that had visited him several times over the last month.

"I'm in the bathroom. I'm looking into the mirror, and suddenly I see a big black bird swooping into the room. I don't know where it's come from or how it's gotten inside. The house lights begin to dim, and then they go off completely. It's pitch black. I'm frightened and run through other rooms, but I hear and feel the flapping wings following me. That's when I wake up frightened, heart pounding, and, strangely, with an electric erection." He grinned at the lilt of his alliteration.

I grinned in return. "Electric erection?"

"It was buzzing, throbbing."

"What hunches do you have about this dream, Alvin? Just let your thoughts run free for a couple minutes. In other words, try to think out loud."

"Pretty obvious. The dream is about death . . . black bird . . . Poe's raven, birds of prey, vultures eating roadkill. . . . I hate vultures and buzzards, and I used to take Jason out with our 22s to pick them off. . . . I remember those shooting expeditions very clearly We did a lot of those. And then the lights in the house dimming . . . I know what that is: it's life fading out. I'm scared to death of death."

"How much do you think about it?"

"Since Jason died, it's on my mind almost every day. Before that, almost never. I remember an eruption of death thoughts and fears when my parents were killed. I was already at Stanford then. I remember the call from my aunt like it was yesterday. I was watching a Warriors-Lakers basketball game on TV."

"How awful, losing both your parents so suddenly."

"It was such a jolt, so sudden, so unexpected. I lived the first two or three weeks stumbling about in a heavy fog. Too much of a shock for tears. And yet, it's strange, after a while I got over it and reentered my life easier than I'm doing now with Jason's death."

"Any ideas why?"

"I think it's because I have no regrets about me and my folks. We all loved one another. They were proud of me, and I was a good son. They lived a full, worthwhile life, were beloved in the community, had a great marriage, and were spared the ravages of old age. I felt clean about them and me. No regrets . . . "

"You paused at 'No regrets.'"

"You don't miss much. Well, I guess there is one regret. I regret that my parents didn't live long enough to see me married and to see their grandkids."

"That's the first mention I've heard about marriage or children. Is that in the cards for you?"

"I always thought so. Not making much progress though."

I tagged that comment, too, for later discussion and pursued the more pressing issue of his grief. "I'm not surprised that your grief over Jason's death has been tougher than grief for your parents. It seems paradoxical, but often we grieve the loss of those with whom we had fulfilled relationships more easily than those with whom so much was unsatisfying, those with whom there was so much unfinished business. After his death, your relationship with Jason was flash-frozen in an unfinished state, never to be resolved. But I want to urge you not to be so hard on yourself. Jason had his own devils pursuing him, and your not having been a good older brother isn't necessarily all about you."

"You mean that Jason played his role in it?"

"That's sure part of it. Being a good older brother requires some cooperation from the younger brother. I'm glad, though, you had that last chance with Jason. Sounds like you really stretched out toward him."

Alvin nodded. "I did all I could. It was tough, reaching out to him with no response. And I felt so alone at his funeral."

"Was there no one you could grieve with?"

"Just a couple of cousins on my paternal side, but I was never close to them. My mother's parents had both died young, and I barely remember my aunts and uncles."

As I dictated my notes after that session, I reviewed the issues I had tagged for later discussion: the death terror manifest in Alvin's nightmare, his expectation of marriage, his self-imposed isolation from both women and men, and his lack of curiosity about that. And that odd "electric erection" at the end of the black bird nightmare.

In the next session, Alvin spoke more of his grief over his parents' death. He recalled the shock when he realized that he had become an orphan. For a while, the thought of moving back to Virginia and taking over his father's practice soothed him, but he soon gave up that plan.

"Living my father's life in Virginia would be like burying myself. I opted to remain in California, but my grief ravaged my sleep. It was terrible for weeks. As soon as I turned off the lights, my heart would start to race, and I'd know there would be no sleep that night. This went on night after night."

"You tried sedatives, of course?"

"I tried everything—even went back to old ones like Seconal, chloral hydrate, Doriden—you name it. Nothing worked."

"How did you resolve it? How long did it take?"

"Eventually . . . " He hesitated for a long time, and his speech became very measured, "Eventually I developed the habit of masturbating in bed. That, uh . . . that was the only thing that worked, and ever since then, I've masturbated every single night. That became my sleeping pill."

Alvin flushed and seemed so uncomfortable that I offered him some breathing room by turning back to the process, to what was happening between the two of us. "I can see how uncomfortable it is for you to speak of this."

"'Uncomfortable' is putting it lightly. I'd say *cosmic embarrassment*. I've never spoken of this to anyone."

"And I want you to know I feel moved by your trust in me. But please, I think it's important to dissect your embarrassment a bit more. You know, embarrassment is never a solitary event.

It always requires at least one other person—in this case, me. I think it emanates from your expectation of how I'd receive your disclosure and how I'd feel about you."

Alvin nodded.

"Can you elaborate on that nod?"

"It's not easy. I thought you'd think I was bizarre—an infant sucking his thumb at night, a creep defiling his family. Yes, a creep: that fits best. And you'd be repelled. And you'd say, 'No wonder you're not going out with women; you're jerking off every night.'"

"None of that, Alvin. Didn't enter my mind. That's not at all where I was. I wasn't judging. I was entirely caught up in trying to understand. My mind was buzzing with ideas. I was thinking of how your heart raced when you turned out the lights at night after your parents' death, and my thoughts went to the connection between sleep and death. I know that many have commented that sleep, losing consciousness, is a little foretaste of death. Did you know that, in Greek mythology, Thanatos and Hypnos—death and sleep—are twin brothers?"

Alvin was listening intently. "No, I didn't know that. Interesting."

"And," I continued, "your comment about being an orphan is so important. I've heard many others who have lost their parents say that. And I know I had the very same thought when my mother died, ten years after my father. When parents die, we always feel vulnerable because we're dealing not only with loss but also with confronting our own death. When we become orphans, there is no one between us and the grave. So I'm not surprised that the death of your whole family has left you feeling exposed and frightened by death and more vulnerable to death anxiety."

"You're saying a whole lot here. You think that, after I turned out the light, my heart began racing because I was experiencing death anxiety?"

"Yes, I do. Remember the light dimming in your black bird nightmare? The presence of darkness sets the stage for awareness of one's own death. And let me say some things that have been on my mind about another part of the puzzle—about your sexual arousal." I knew I was saying much too much at one time here, but after I got started, I couldn't stop. "I think of sex as the vital antagonist to death—isn't the orgasm the primal spark of life? I know of many instances in which sexual feelings arise in order to neutralize fears of death. That protective process, I think, produced the 'electric erection' at the end of your nightmare and explains your use of masturbation as a way of soothing yourself to ward off death anxiety so you can fall asleep."

"These are all new thoughts to me, Irv. A little too much to take in at one time."

"And I don't expect you to. It's important we go over this again and again. In my field this is what we mean by 'working it through.'"

Over the next sessions, I continued to address, in a candid manner, his concerns about death. I did a detailed death anamnesis, in which he related all of his early memories of death. I asked him, for example, when he first apprehended the idea of death.

He thought for a minute or two. "I was about five or six, I guess, when our collie, Max, was hit by a car. I remember crying and running into my father's office, in the front room of our house. My father grabbed his black bag, rushed outside, and leaned down to examine Max, who was lying by the curb. My father shook his head and said there was nothing he could do. That was when I got it. I got that death couldn't be fixed. Not even by my father, who could fix almost anything.

"Another time, a few years later, maybe seventh grade, my teacher, Mrs. Thurston, told us that Ralph, a boy in my class—my age, a kid like me—had died of polio. Still, today, I see Ralph's face clearly, his large ears, bristle-brush hair always standing at attention, bright brown eyes full of wonder. But here's the curious thing: I wasn't that close to Ralph. I never saw him outside of school. He lived far away, and his mother drove him to school. But I walked, with several other classmates. And I played with those kids all the time. Yet it is Ralph's face I see. I can't see the others."

"Interesting," I said. "I suspect that Ralph's face remains so clearly etched in your memory because it's linked to some strong subterranean thoughts about death."

Alvin nodded. "Hard to argue with that. I'm sure that is so. In Sunday school, the grown-ups talked of heaven, and I remember asking Dad about it. He dismissed the thought. He called it a fairy tale. He was a materialist—like most physicians, I think. His view was that when the brain goes, the mind goes, and along with it all awareness and perception, everything. Death is simply 'lights out.' You agree?"

I nodded. "I'm with your dad on that: I can't imagine a disembodied consciousness."

We sat in silence for a while. It was a good moment. I felt close to Alvin. "What did your dad's answer mean to you? Did it diminish your anxiety about death?"

"No, it offered no solace. The idea of everything ending, or at least ending for me, was something I just couldn't get my mind around."

Alvin and I worked through these issues for several sessions. We reviewed them from different angles, we considered additional confirmatory memories, we explored some new, relevant dreams, and we solidified our gains. Gradually, however, therapy began to slow down. I always think therapy is working well when patients take risks each session, but Alvin took no further risks, and we broke no new ground. Soon, right on schedule, Alvin began to question what we were doing.

"I'm puzzled about your approach. I'm losing sight of exactly where we're going. Are we trying to help eliminate my death anxiety? After all, don't we all dread death? Don't you?"

"Of course I do. The fear of death is hardwired into all of us. It enables us to survive. Those who were wired without that trait were winnowed out eons ago. So, no, I'm not aiming at removing fear, but for you, Alvin, that fear has morphed into something greater, into a terror that haunts you in your recurring nightmares and intrudes into your daily work. Am I right?"

"Well, not exactly. I'm noticing that I am changing a bit. Maybe I'm better. No more nightmares; I'm OK at work now; I rarely think of Jason anymore. So what next? I wonder if we're about finished?"

That question arises often in therapy when symptoms diminish and patients regain their previous equilibrium. Is it really time to stop? Is it enough simply to remove the symptoms? Or should we reach for more? Should we not try to alter the patient's underlying character and lifestyle that have given birth to these symptoms? I tried to be tactful as I gently guided Alvin toward further exploration: "Ultimately, Alvin, the decision as to whether you're finished and ready to stop rests with you. But I think we shouldn't fail to take a closer look at what's helped you to improve. If we can identify the helpful factors, you may be able to call upon them in the future."

"What's helped? Tough question. For sure, something about talking to you has helped. But how? I'd be only guessing. Maybe just getting things out, revealing some things for the first time. For sure, knowing you were genuinely interested helped me. I haven't had that feeling with anyone since my dad died."

"Yes, I sensed that. And I felt that you took some real risks and made good use of our time together." So far, so good, I thought, and then attempted to go further. "But now I think we're ready to do more. I think it's important to explore why you've arranged your life in the way you have. You have good social skills, you seem comfortable in your skin, and you say you benefit from the intimacy with me. So my question is, why have you backed away from the possibility of intimacy with others? What's the payoff in living in such isolation?"

Alvin obviously did not appreciate my inquiry and shook his head as I spoke. "Look, there's a continuum from private to public. Some folks are extroverts by nature, and some simply prefer to remain private. I guess I'm just at the 'private' end of the continuum. I *like* being alone."

There it was. In therapy lingo, *resistance* had made its entry. I persevered, though I knew he was digging in his heels. "Yet just a few minutes ago you talked about how comforting it was for you to speak intimately to me and to experience my interest in you."

"That's true, but I don't need it all the time."

The hour came to an end, and as we stopped, Alvin said, "I don't think we're getting anywhere."

As I thought about our session, I marveled at how quickly things had changed. Until this session, Alvin and I had been allies in every way, yet now, suddenly, we seemed to be on opposing sides. No, as I thought more about what had happened, I knew that Alvin's deep resistance wasn't a complete surprise; I'd had a foreshadowing of it earlier when my exploration of his relationships with women had always fizzled out so quickly. I remembered his refusal to engage that question, and I recalled puzzling at his lack of curiosity about himself. In fact, a prominent lack of curiosity is generally a road sign telling a therapist that a patient may be unwilling to explore more deeply. I knew this was not going to be easy.

The struggle continued through the next session. The strength of his refusal to look at his social withdrawal convinced me that there were powerful forces in play. I'd seen many isolated, withdrawn individuals before, but rarely anyone with such competent social skills and capacity for intimacy. I was baffled. There was something odd going on.

"Let me share something, Alvin. In one of our first meetings, when you told me about your twenty-four-hour schedule, I felt some sadness for you. There seems so little warmth or human touch in your life. That somehow doesn't fit with the Alvin I know, not with your forthrightness or your capacity for intimacy. And it doesn't fit with the type of home life you had growing up. I know there were problems with your brother; still, you describe your parents as caring and nurturing and modeling a loving relationship and partnership. Individuals with your kind of background don't cut themselves off from others in adulthood."

"I'll grant there are changes I should make, and I will get around to them."

I kept trying to chip away, "Yet time keeps flowing on. I recall your saying that, ten years ago, when your parents died, you felt regret that they'd never seen you married or known their grand-children. What about those regrets? And what are your regrets for yourself? Are you living the life you've hoped to live?"

"As I say, I will get around to making changes. But it's not front and center for me now. Remember why I came to you. I came because of my anxiety following my brother's death. My social life has got nothing to do with that."

I took the last arrow out of my quiver, "I don't agree. There's a strong connection between the two. Let me try to explain. I've observed again and again that the amount of death ter-ror experienced is closely related to the amount of life unlived. And *that's* the reason that I'm trying to focus on the quality of your life now."

As though I had hit a resonant chord, Alvin sank into deep thought for a minute, but then he responded, "Perhaps at some later time. I'm doing OK at present and feel disinclined to pur-sue it now."

Analyze the resistance, analyze the resistance—that's my mantra when I encounter such an impasse. I persisted: "During our first several hours together I was so impressed with your willingness to examine your responses to your brother's death, and by your courage in sharing intimate aspects of your life. I had a sense of our working well together. But in these last sessions, we've really hit a wall. You're balking at going further, but I'm absolutely convinced that you know there's more to do. It's as though you no longer trust me."

"No, that last part's not true."

"Then help me understand what's happened. At what point do you feel things changed here?"

"It's not you, Irv; it's me. Look, there are just some things I'm not ready to discuss."

"I know this feels like badgering, but indulge me a bit further. Let me make one last inquiry. I have a hunch that the blockage you're feeling is related to your relationships with women. Earlier you described your relationships as just fizzling out. I'm wondering if that had to do with the sexual aspect of those relationships."

"No, that's not the issue."

"Then what *is* the issue?" I knew I was out of line. I was almost battering my patient, but I couldn't stop. My curiosity was aflame and had taken on a life of its own.

To my surprise, Alvin opened the door a crack. "I meet a lot of terrific women, and the same thing happens every time. We go out, have dinner, sex is great, we like one another, and then sooner or later, after a few dates, the women come to my house. And then it ends."

"Why? What happens?"

"Once they see my house, I never see them again."

"Why? What do they see?" I was still clueless and feeling oddly slow on the uptake.

"They get upset. Don't like what they see. Don't like the way I take care of my house."

Alvin and I both looked at the clock. We had run over a few minutes. He wanted out of the office, and I had a patient waiting. I took a risk.

"I'm really glad you're trusting me with this. I'm going to make an unusual proposal that I think might be tremendously important for your therapy. I'd like to hold our next session at your house. Can you make it a week from today at six pm?"

Alvin took a deep breath and tried to relax. "I'm not sure. I need to think about it. Let me sleep on it and phone you tomorrow."

"Sure, call me here between seven and ten in the morning." That was my writing time, which I ordinarily hold inviolate. But this was really important.

At one minute past seven the next morning, Alvin called: "Irv, I can't handle this. I was up all night stewing. I just can't deal with your visiting me at home, and I can't deal with more sleepless nights waiting for next week. I want to stop therapy."

A lot of things flashed through my mind. I'd been around long enough to know that many patients require repeated courses of therapy. They do some work, make some changes, and then terminate. After therapy stops, they consolidate their gains for months or years, and then, at some future point, they return for additional, often more comprehensive work. Any mature therapist would recognize that pattern and show restraint. But I wasn't feeling particularly mature.

"Alvin, I feel certain that you're upset by envisioning my response to your home. Perhaps you feel a lot of shame; perhaps you worry about my feelings toward you?"

"I can't deny that's part of it."

"I have a sense your thought is divided. You've alluded to one part, the part overwhelmed by shame. But there is also the part that wants to change. That's the part that decided to tell me about the nature of your problem, the part that really wants to live in a different way. And that's the part of you I want to engage. You don't have to wait a week. Let's meet today. What's your schedule this morning? I could come right now."

"No, it's too much for me."

"Alvin, you're turning down an opportunity to set your life on a different, more satisfying course, and I think you're rejecting that option because of your fears of my judging you. But you've already learned those fears are unfounded. And, second, let me ask you to take a cosmic perspective: you're allowing a fear of some fleeting feeling passing through my mind to influence the entire course of your one and only life. Does that make sense?"

"Okay, Irv, you're wearing me down. But I can't do it now. I'm just leaving for work, and I'm scheduled wall-to-wall today."

"What time are you done?"

"About seven this evening."

"How about I come over at seven thirty for a session?"

"Are you sure this is the right thing?"

"Trust me. I'm sure."

Promptly at seven thirty, I arrived at his attractive small home in Sunnyvale, a few miles from my Palo Alto office. The front door was ajar, and scotch-taped to it was a note that read, "Come right in." I rang the doorbell and entered. At the far end of the living room, in a large lounge chair, Alvin sat facing a window. I could see only the back of his head. He did not turn toward me.

I wanted to go to Alvin, but I wasn't sure how to reach him. I could not see more than a few, very small sections of bare floor. The remainder of its surface was covered entirely by tall stacks of old telephone books—where had he gotten them all?—large art books, books of train schedules, stacks of yellowed newspapers, and piles of old science fiction books. I love science fiction and restrained myself from sitting down on a *New York Times* tumulus to start browsing. The only places I could see the hardwood floor were narrow, perhaps ten-inch-wide trails, one leading to the adjoining kitchen, another to Alvin's chair, and a third to a large sofa covered with more dusty books and heaps of old x-ray films and medical charts.

The year was 1982, and hoarding had yet appeared as a familiar topic in psychiatry or on daytime television. I had never before seen or imagined anything like the inside of Alvin's home. Feeling too overcome to manage a foray into other rooms, I cautiously weaved my way over to the chair nearest Alvin and sat down, facing his back.

"Alvin," I spoke loudly, the chairs being fifteen feet apart, "thank you for meeting with me here. It is important that you've allowed me to see your home, and I feel now, more than ever, that we need to continue to meet. I know how hard this is for you, and I appreciate your allowing me into your life and your home."

Alvin nodded but remained silent.

I was at a loss for words. I knew that eventually we would attempt to understand the hoarding by working on its meaning and its genesis, but at this moment, it was imperative that we examine our relationship, now roiling with humiliation and anger.

"Alvin, I'm so sorry to put you through this, but there is no other way. We have to face this together. I know this is hard for you, but it's a big step forward—a huge step—and we need to talk it through. I'm wondering if there's a place where we can sit closer to talk."

Alvin shook his head.

"Or perhaps we can stroll around the block?"

"Not now, Irv, this is all I can do today, and I want to stop."

"Well then, tomorrow. Can you make it at this same time, seven thirty, tomorrow evening, in my office?"

Alvin nodded. "I'll phone you first thing in the morning."

I sat for a few more minutes in silence and then left.

The next morning, Alvin phoned. I was not surprised by his words, "Irv, I'm sorry, but I simply can't make it. Don't think I don't appreciate what you've done, but I can't meet again. At least not now."

"Alvin, I know I've pushed you hard—too hard perhaps—but look at what we've done. We're on the brink of something crucial."

"Nope. Not now. We're done. Perhaps I'll call you in the future. For now I can deal with it on my own. I'll start to organize my home."

I closed Alvin's folder. Since that visit to his house I had not seen him or heard from him until the previous day at Molly's funeral. And what was he doing there anyway? What was his connection with Molly? I recall that for some time after our last visit I thought about Alvin and wondered about what had happened to him, and while walking through the corridors or sitting in the hospital cafeteria, I scanned my surroundings looking for him. I remember, also, following my last session with him, speaking at some length with an old and close friend, also a psychiatrist, to help me deal with my own dismay at having so badly bungled a case. But now, after our meeting at Molly's memorial yesterday, I had to reconsider. Had I bungled it? Alvin looked great and had two children and a lovely wife, who told me that I was responsible for their marriage. How had that all come about? I must have been more effective than I thought. My curiosity once again was aflame.

* * *

We met for coffee at a small café near the hospital, taking a corner table for privacy.

"Sorry," I began, "that I was a bit slow to recognize you. As I mentioned, aging has taken its toll on my facial recognition. But don't think I haven't thought about you, Alvin. I've often wondered about how you've fared, especially since I thought our work together ended prematurely, leaving you with problems still to work on. I'd love a follow-up. You know, I think I didn't recognize you at first yesterday because I hadn't expected to see you at Molly's funeral. How did you know Molly?"

A look of surprise appeared on Alvin's face. "Don't you remember? A day or two after our last session you called and gave me her name and suggested I contact her to help me get my house back in order."

"Oh, my, I had entirely forgotten that. And you *did* contact her?"

Alvin nodded vigorously. "Oh yes. You mean, she never mentioned me to you?"

"She wouldn't. She had her honor code: she was tight-lipped as a clam about identifying her clients. But I referred you to her over thirty years ago. You still remember her from back then?"

"No, that's not quite it. What happened is that I called Molly immediately, and she took over. I mean took over completely. In a few days my house was neater than it had ever been, and she has taken care of my house and my bills, my taxes, and *all* my affairs ever since. I was her client right up till her death. I've often told Monica how grateful I am to you. You turned my life around. You gave me so much. But, most of all, you gave me Molly. All these years, the past thirty years, she's come to my house once a week without fail and taken care of everything until just a couple of months ago, when she grew too ill. She was the best thing that ever came my way—except, of course, for Monica and my two wonderful children."

After our conversation, my mind swirled with thoughts about the impossibility of ever learning how psychotherapy works. We therapists strive so fervently for precision in our work and aspire to be fine-tuned empiricists, trying to offer precise fixes for the broken elements in our patients' attachment history or DNA sequences. Yet the realities of our work do not fit that model, and often we find ourselves improvising as we and our patients stumble together on the journey toward recovery. I used to be unnerved by that, but now, in my golden years, I whistle softly to myself as I marvel at the complexities and unpredictability of human thought and behavior. Now, rather than being rattled by uncertainty, I realize that it is pure hubris to posit specificity. Now, the one thing I've come to know with certainty is that if I can create a genuine and caring environment, my patients will find the help they need, often in marvelous ways I could never have predicted or even imagined. Thank you, Molly.

~ 5 ~

Don't Fence Me In

Dear Dr. Yalom

I'm a seventy-seven year old (former) CEO and a year ago I moved into a retirement home in Georgia. Nice place but it's not working out: I'm having severe and persistent adjustment problems. I've been seeing a therapist for the past year but our work has recently bogged down. Can you see me in consultation? I'm willing to fly to California at any time.

Rick Evans

Three weeks later Rick Evans strode confidently into my office appearing as though he had been there often. He looked the way I think a retired CEO should look: lean, attractive, relaxed. With his bronze golfer's tan, his regal posture, his masterfully chiseled nose and chin, I could picture him on the brochure cover for any upscale retirement community. And his thick shock of straight, neatly parted, gleaming white hair was a wonder to behold. I ran my hand dolefully over my own balding scalp. Though I couldn't catch his glance full on, I liked his intense yet slightly plaintive eyes.

Rick wasted no time, speaking even as he was taking his seat. "That book of yours, *Staring at the Sun: Overcoming the Terror of Death* is strong, very strong. Especially for someone my age. That book is why I'm here."

He glanced at his watch as though checking that we were starting on time. "Let me get right to the point. As I mentioned in my email, I moved into Fairlawn Oaks a year ago. After my wife died, I first tried to make a go of it at my home. Tried like hell for eighteen months, but couldn't do it, not even with a lot of household help. Just too damn much hassle with all the shopping, the cooking, the cleaning. And it was too damn lonely. So I made the move. But it's not working out. Not that I'm knocking Fairlawn Oaks. The home is great. But I'm just not adapting."

I was struck by all Rick had *not* done. He had not looked around at my office—not even for an instant—nor had he made any social gesture of greeting. He had come all the way across the country to see me and yet had not once cast his eyes in my direction. Perhaps he was more anxious than he appeared. Perhaps he was entirely task-oriented and intent only on making the most efficient use of his time. I'd get back to all that later. For now, I encouraged him to continue his story.

"Not adapting how?"

He flicked off my inquiry with a twitch of his wrist. "I'll tell you about that. But first I want to say something about the therapist I've been seeing for a year and a half. She's a good lady. She helped with my grief, no question about it. She got me up from the floor, sponged me off, and back into the ring, back into the world. But now we've stalled. Not blaming her, but in our therapy hours we're wasting time and money, though she doesn't charge your high-end rates. We're just going around in a circle, covering the same stuff over and over again. Then, after reading your book, I read some of your others, too, and suddenly had the thought that a consultation with you could give my therapy a jump-start." Even here he didn't look at me. This felt odd, as he certainly was not a shy man. He just plowed right ahead. "Now, I know therapists are possessive and touchy about that sort of thing, so I decided to run it by her in a diplomatic fashion. Don't get me wrong: I wasn't asking her permission. I was going to contact you whatever she said. Turned out she was very positive. She grabbed at the thought: 'Sure, sure, good idea. Contact him for a consultation. I'd welcome that. California's a long way off, but what better use for your time and money?' She offered to write you a note describing our therapy work, but I felt a bit miffed and told her I was a big boy and I could take care of filling you in."

"Miffed? Why?" It was time to push myself into this monologue.

"I'm old but not helpless. I can figure out how to contact you by myself."

"That's all? That worth a miff? Go deeper." I felt impelled to be more confrontational than is my wont.

Rick's cadence slowed. Maybe now, finally, he had taken note of me, though he still hadn't really looked at me. "Well, I don't know. Maybe miffed at her being just a tad too happy at the thought of possibly getting rid of me. Maybe I *wanted* her to be a little possessive. But I get your point. I know my getting miffed isn't rational. After all, she and I are using this consultation with you to help us continue our work together. She's not trying to get rid of me, and she said as much. But I'm leveling with you. That's the way I felt. Miffed. I'm not going to hold anything back today. I want my money's worth out of this investment. You know, with your fee and the airfare, this adds up."

"Tell me about your adjustment to the retirement home."

"In a minute." Once again, he flicked me away. "First let me get on record and make it clear that Fairlawn Oaks is great. It's a damn good organization, and if I were running it, I don't think there's much I'd change. My problems are all my own stuff—I acknowledge it. Fairlawn Oaks has it all. The meals are fine, and they offer a ton of terrific activities. The golf course is a bit tame, yet at my age it's just right. But here's the thing: all day long I am crippled with ambivalence. Every time I start to do something, my mind starts wanting to do something else. Now I don't do schedules—at least not other people's schedules—that's not who I am. Schedules are for others. Why *must* I go to the swimming pool exercise class at four pm every day? Or to the current events class at ten am? Why *must* I put the door key in that pouch on the door *every* time? And why *must* I have meals at the same time every day? That's not me. The real me, the real Rick Evans, reveres spontaneity."

He turned his head in my direction. "You went right from college to medical school, right?"

"Right."

"And then into psychiatry, right?"

"Yep."

"Well, I've had nine professions." He held up nine fingers. "Nine! And did damn well in all nine. Started with nothing as a printer's apprentice. . . . Then I became a printer . . . then started a magazine . . . then a publisher of several magazines . . . then head of a small textbook publishing company . . . then bought and built up a string of board and care places for the mentally disturbed . . . then ran a hospital, and then, believe it or not, took training as a counselor and went into organizational development work . . . and then CEO of two different companies." He sat back in his chair looking satisfied. It was my turn to say something. I had no particular plan in mind but began responding anyway, hoping my muse would guide me.

"A lot of different paths. Hard to register them all. Tell me, Rick—OK if we use first names? Call me Irv?"

Rick nodded. "I prefer it."

"Rick, how do you feel now when you look back on your careers?"

"Look, be assured that none of these moves was forced. I never failed with any of these careers. I just got fidgety after a while. I refuse to be locked into any way of life. I require change. Spontaneity. I repeat: *spontaneity*—that's who I am!"

"And now?"

"Now? Well, that's the whole point. Spontaneity, once a good thing, once my strength, my polestar, has now morphed into a monster. Look, here's the picture: when I start to head off to some activity, be it fitness training, pool aerobics, current events, yoga classes, whatever, my mind starts rattling off other alternatives. I hear my inner voice asking, 'Why *this* activity?

Why not some *other* activity?' I'm stuck in a logjam of indecision. And what happens? What happens is I end up doing none of these activities."

I checked into my own flow of thoughts. As Rick spoke, I thought of Buridan's ass, an ancient philosophical paradox involving an ass placed between two equally sweet-smelling bales of hay, who starves to death because he can't decide which one to choose. But I saw no benefit to Rick in speaking of this. I'd be just responding to his challenging manner and showing off my erudition. Then another thought occurred that might be more acceptable and more useful to him. "Rick, let me share something that's just drifted into my mind."

I knew I was being a bit loose, but that often paid off—patients generally appreciate my sharing something of myself, and it usually works to accelerate more sharing. "Maybe it will be of interest. It's an episode that occurred long ago. I wrote about it somewhere but haven't thought about it in ages. One day, I noted that my eyeglasses weren't functioning properly, and I paid a visit to my ophthalmologist, a much older man. After he tested my vision, he asked my age. 'Forty,' I responded. 'Forty, eh?' he said, and he took off his own glasses, wiped them carefully, and said, 'Well, young man, you're right on schedule. Presbyopia.' I remember feeling very annoyed and wanting to say to him, 'What schedule? Who's on schedule? You or your other patients may be on schedule but not me! Not me! I'm different.'"

"Nice story," Rick replied. "I read it somewhere in one of your books. I get your point, but actually it's not really *my* point. I already know the math. I'm seventy-seven, and we don't need to waste time working on that. I'm not in denial anymore. Not only do I tell myself every day that I'm seventy-seven, but my one-note therapist keeps hammering it home. My unwillingness to confront my age was what made it so difficult to leave my home and move into Fairlawn. But I've moved on. I'm talking about something new."

Hmm, it was clear that sharing my eyeglasses story had not been a great idea. Rick was not someone with whom I could be loose and share associations that float into my mind. He was more invested in competing with me than being helped by me. I decided to keep a sharper focus.

"Rick, earlier you said, 'Spontaneity—that's who I am.'"

"That's right. It's my mantra. That is who I am."

"*That is who I am*," I repeated. "If we transpose that statement, it becomes 'If I am not spontaneous, I am not me.'"

"Yes, I guess so. Sounds cute, I guess, but . . . your point?"

"Well, that thought has dark implications. It's a close cousin to saying to yourself, 'If I am not spontaneous, I won't exist.'"

"I won't exist as *me*, as the core person I am."

"I'm guessing it runs even deeper. It's as though you believe your spontaneity wards off your death."

"I know these pronouncements are meant to be helpful, but I'm not getting it. You're saying that? . . ." he held out his hands, palms facing me, fingers splayed.

"I'm wondering if, at some deeper level, you might feel that giving up your spontaneity is risky, that it brings death closer. I mean, if we look at your situation rationally, we'd ask, 'What's the real threat in doing some things on schedule?' At seventy-seven putting your keys in some designated place makes sense.

I sure need to do that. And obviously it makes sense to go to exercise classes or current events discussion at a certain time because a group's existence requires a designated time to get together."

"I'm not claiming that my thought is rational. I grant that it doesn't make sense."

"But it *does* make sense if we assume it is powered by some deep, not entirely conscious fear. I think that being 'on schedule' symbolizes, to you, marching in lockstep with everyone else toward death. Fairlawn Oaks can't help but be connected in your mind with the end of life, and your inability—or, rather, *unwillingness*—to engage in the program must be a form of unconscious protest."

"Pretty far-fetched. Sounds like you're really stretching. Just because I don't want to line up, towel in hand, to do water exercises with all the other old ninnies doesn't mean that I refuse to accept my mortality. I don't do lines. I'm not about to get into any kind of line."

"I'm not getting into any kind of line because? . . ." I asked.

"I designate lines; I don't stand in them."

"In other words, I don't get into lines because I'm special."

"Damn right. That's why I told you about my nine careers."

"Stretching, expanding, actualizing yourself: all these endeavors seem right. They seem appropriate for a certain time of life. But perhaps they may not fit *this* time of life."

"*You're* still working."

"So what questions do you have for me?"

"Well, why do *you* work? Are you really in step with *your* age?"

"Fair enough. Let me try to answer. We all face aging in our own manner. I know I'm very old. There is no denying that eighty is old. I'm working less—I see far fewer patients now, only about three a day, but I'm still writing much of the rest of the day. I'll tell you the truth: I love what I'm doing. I feel blessed to be of help to others, especially others who are facing the issues I'm dealing with—aging, retirement, dealing with the death of a spouse or friends, contemplating my own death."

For the first time Rick did not respond but silently looked at the floor.

"Your feelings about my answer," I asked in a softer voice.

"I got to hand it to you. You go right into the tough stuff. Death of friends, your own death."

"And your thoughts of death. Is it much on your mind?"

Rick shook his head. "I don't think about it. Why would I? Wouldn't do any good."

"Sometimes thoughts enter the mind involuntarily in day-dreams, for example, or night dreams."

"Dreams? I don't dream much . . . none for weeks . . . but strangely I had two doozies last night."

"Tell me all you remember." I picked up my notepad. Two dreams just before our session. I had a hunch these were going to be illuminating.

"In the first one I was at a school playground with a big chain-link fence around the field—"

"Rick, let me interrupt. Would you mind describing the dream in the present tense—as though you're just now seeing it."

"Okay. Here goes. I'm in a school playground—maybe my junior high school field—and there's a baseball game getting organized. I look around and see that everyone there is much younger. They're all kids—adolescents—in uniform. I want to play—I really do—but I feel strange because I'm too big. Then I see the teacher. . . . He looks familiar, but I can't place him. I start to approach him to ask what to do, and just then I notice another area of the playground where several older people—my age—are organizing another game—maybe golf, maybe croquet—not sure which. I start to join them, but I can't get past the fence surrounding the ball field."

"Hunches about this dream, Rick? Tell me anything that comes to mind."

"Well, baseball. I used to love playing when I was young. My favorite sport. I was good at it. Shortstop with a helluva peg. Could have played college ball, maybe even pro, but I had to go to work. My parents had no money."

"Keep going. Say more about the dream."

"Well, kids were playing, and I wanted to play. But I'm not a kid anymore."

"Feelings about that? Or other feelings you had in that dream?"

"Yeah, my therapist never fails to ask that question. I don't recall any feelings. But let me try—*happy* when I first saw the ball game—that's one feeling. And then some *aching* and *bafflement* when I saw I couldn't play. If you want feelings, though, the other dream last night had some stronger feelings. Lots of aggravation and frustration. In that dream I was . . . I am in the bathroom looking at myself in the mirror, but it is all blurred, as though the mirror is steamed over. I have a spray bottle of cleaner, and I keep squeezing the last spurts in the bottle, and I keep rubbing and cleaning the mirror, but it just will not get clear."

"Isn't it strange that you hadn't dreamed for months before—"

"I said '*weeks*.'"

"Sorry, you haven't dreamed for *weeks*, and then last night, the very night before we meet, you have these two strong dreams. It's as though you dreamt them for our session today, as though your unconscious is sending us some clues to the mystery."

"God, the way you guys think—my unconscious sending mysterious messages to my conscious for my shrink to decode. You can't be serious."

"Well, let's examine this together. Think of the major problem you bring here, that you can't adjust to your community, that you are shackled by alternative desires. That you end up frozen, not doing anything. Right?"

"Yeah, I'm with you."

"Surely the first dream speaks to that. Keep in mind that dreams are almost entirely visual and convey meaning only through visual images. So look at the picture your dream offers of your life dilemma. You want to play baseball, the game you loved as a kid, the game you had great talent for, but you can't join that game because of your age. There's another game there for folks your age, but you can't join that game because you can't get past the fence around the ball field. So, you're too old for one game and fenced out of the other. Right?"

"Right. Yeah, yeah, I see your point. Well, perhaps it *is* saying I don't really know my age. It's saying I'm foolish by thinking that I'm young enough to play in the baseball game. I don't belong there."

"And the other game?"

"Behind that fence? That part's not as clear."

"Still see the fence in your mind's eye?"

"Yep."

"Keep looking at it, and just let thoughts about that fence drift into your mind."

"Plain old chain-link fence. Used to look through them when I was a kid to watch the older kids playing ball. And oh, yes, we had a class B minor league team in our town, and there was a little slit in the fence in center field where we use to watch the games before we got chased away. Ordinary fence— see 'em everywhere."

"If that fence could speak to you, what would it say?"

"Hmm, a little Fritz Perls technique, huh? I remember that from my counseling program."

"Right you are. Fritz knew a thing or two about dreams. Keep going. What might the fence say?"

"Uh, damnedest thing happening."

"What?"

"Well, I hear a tune playing in my mind right now. 'Don't Fence Me In.' You know that song?"

"I think I remember a bit of it."

"Here's the thing. Last week that tune invaded my mind for hours, and I couldn't get away from it. It just kept playing like background music. I tried to remember all the words but couldn't and finally went to YouTube and found a video of Roy Rogers riding his horse, Trigger, and singing that song. Great lyrics! Then, when I saw a computer ad to get the melody of that song as the ring tone on my cell phone, I was tempted to order it and clicked on it. I nixed it when I saw they were going to charge some goddamned outrageous monthly fee."

"Remember some of the lyrics?"

"You bet." Rick closed his eyes and sang softly:

Oh, give me land, lots of land under starry skies above
Don't fence me in
Let me ride through the wide open country that I love
Don't fence me in
Let me be by myself in the evenin' breeze
And listen to the murmur of the cottonwood trees
Send me off forever, but I ask you please
Don't fence me in

"Great, Rick. Thanks. Lot of heart in your singing. Those lyrics—'Don't fence me in'—really do speak to your life predicament. And I get a kick out of thinking of you having a phone ring tone with that melody. I wonder if it would help."

"It sure would keep my predicament front and center. No hints about the solution, though."

"Let's turn to the other dream—the mirror that you kept cleaning? And the spray bottle's last spurts? Any hunches?"

Rick flashed a big smile. "You're making me do all the work."

"It's your dream. You're the guy, the only one who can do it."

"Well, my image in the mirror is blurred. I know what you're going to say."

"What?" I raised my chin.

"You're going to say that I don't know myself, that my own image is blurred to myself."

"Yep, probably what I *would* say. And the last spurts?"

"No mystery there. I'm seventy-seven."

"Exactly, you're trying to get yourself into focus but can't do it, can't make the image sharper, and it's getting late. I'm impressed by your effort in the dream and your effort in coming all this distance to see me. Seems as though there is a powerful desire within you to know yourself, to sharpen your focus. I admire that."

Rick looked up and finally caught my gaze.

"How did *that* feel?" I asked.

"How did what feel?"

"What you just did. Looking at me. Looking into my eyes."

"I don't understand what you're getting at."

"It seems to me that this was the first time you really looked at me, the first time we really touched."

"Never thought of therapy consultation as a social hour. Where's this coming from?"

"It was that statement you made earlier, 'I was too damned lonely.' I was wondering how lonely you've been feeling in this room with me."

"I don't think about that. But I admit you've got a point. There are people all around me, but I just don't connect."

"It would help me understand more if you'd take me through a twenty-four-hour day. Pick a typical day last week."

"Well, I have breakfast . . . "

"What time do you wake up?"

"About six."

"And your typical night's sleep?"

"Probably six to seven hours. I go to bed around eleven and read myself to sleep around eleven thirty or eleven forty-five. Get up to take a leak about two or three times."

"And you mentioned you don't dream often."

"I rarely remember dreams. My therapist's been on my case about that. Tells me that everyone dreams every night."

"And breakfast?"

"I get to the dining room early. I like that because I can sit alone and read the paper with breakfast. The rest of the day you already know about. I torment myself about going or not going to activities. If the weather's good, I take a walk alone for at least an hour. And I often take lunch in my room alone. But then at dinner you can't sit alone. They seat you with others, so I put on a good act of socializing."

"Evenings?"

"TV, or sometimes a film at Fairlawn. Most of the evenings alone."

"Tell me about the main people in your life right now."

"I spend a lot more time avoiding people than meeting people. A lot of single women there, but it's awkward. If I get too friendly with one, then she'll be looking for me at every meal and every activity. If you get involved with one, there's no chance you can date another without hell to pay."

"How about people you knew before you went into the retirement community?"

"I have a son. He's a banker living in London, and he phones or, lately, Skypes every Sunday morning. Good kid. Two grandchildren—a boy and a girl. And that's about it. Lost touch with everyone else from my former life. My wife and I had a lively social life, but she was the hub. She organized everything, and I just went along."

"It's curious, isn't it? You say you're lonely, yet you have such good social skills, and you're surrounded by people whom you try to avoid."

"Doesn't make sense, I know. But not sure how this is connected to my problem about spontaneity and indecision."

"Perhaps there is more than one problem. Perhaps, as we proceed, some connection will emerge. What strikes me is your strong focus on task and your inattention to relationship. Your description of your dilemma about your activities at Fairlawn involves only the nature of the activity, but no mention of other people. Who'll be there? Who's guiding the activity? Who would you like to hang out with? And we had a small taste of that here today as you focused only on getting started quickly and being efficient but sought no real encounter with me. You never inquired about who I was or what I had to offer. Until I invited you to question me, you expressed no interest in me."

"I did say I read your book and already had an introduction to you there."

"Right. But your relationship to me was private and excluded me."

"Come on, this sounds silly. I'm here to get something from you. I'm paying you for your services. I'll most likely never see you again. What's the point in social make-believe?"

"Earlier you mentioned your training program as a counselor. Right?"

"Yeah, two-year training program."

"You remember that the interview, like our interview today, consists of both process and content? Content is obvious—it's the information exchanged. The *process*—that is, the relationship between interviewer and interviewee—gives you even more relevant information, in that you get a glimpse of the client's behavior toward others. It's important because the interview situation is a microcosm of the client's behavior with other people. So *that's* what I'm noting. That's why I'm commenting about the absence of connection between us until that moment you caught my glance."

"So you're saying that my behavior here tells you about my behavior with others."

I nodded.

"Sometimes I think shrinks place too much importance on relationships. There are other things in the world. I'm not craving to meet others. I'm getting along fine without them. Some folks prefer solitude."

"You're right. I *do* make the assumption that relationships are central. I believe we're embedded in them, and we all do better in the presence of an intimate nourishing relationship. Like that long, good, loving one you had with your wife."

"Well, that's gone, and, frankly, I don't have the energy to begin again."

"Or maybe you don't ever want to face that kind of loss and pain again. No relationships, no pain."

Rick nodded. "Yep, I've thought of that."

"You end up protecting yourself, but the cost is high. You cut yourself off from so much. And let me repeat this: even your quandary of 'Which activity?' might lose its power if you put 'Which people?' into the equation."

"Right. I never think of that. You may have a point, but I think you've glossed over my original concern, my devotion to *spontaneity*. You just writing that off?"

"No, I've been thinking about it the whole time we've been talking. I personally treasure spontaneity. I rely on it when I write. I value being pulled by something unexpected and going off into unpredictable directions. In fact, I love that. But I don't think much of your behavior is now propelled by spontaneity, that is, being pulled by something outside yourself. You're not being pulled, but, instead, you're being pushed by some force inside that is trying to escape fear or danger."

"Can you translate that into plainer language?"

"I'll try. Let me put it this way. I think there is a sense of great danger lurking within you that is corrupting your natural spontaneity. You said yourself that your spontaneity had morphed into a monster. You're not being pulled by some goal. Instead your actions seem aimed at warding off some internal danger."

"What internal danger?"

"Afraid I'm only going to be repeating myself, but I don't know how else to say it. The danger is mortality, the danger confronting all of us. It lies in your dealing with the knowledge that if your wife dies, then so shall you. The retirement home, however lovely, is also foreboding, and you experience it as a trap, a final stop, as a prison confining you, and you don't want to go along with any part of its schedule."

I could see him shaking his head ever so slightly. "I've never thought of it as a prison. It's run damn well, and I can leave anytime I choose."

I knew I wasn't getting through. I glanced at my watch. "And speaking of schedules, Rick, we're up against one today, and I'm afraid our time together is running out. I know you're left perplexed, but will you think about all I've said and get back to me by email and let me know if any of this clicks for you later? My hope is that our session will give you food for thought and help get your therapy unstuck."

"I'll think on it all right. It's a bit of a jumble now. But I'll mull on it, and I'll write. Are you available for another session, say in a few months, in case I want to repeat this course?"

"If I'm here, I'll be glad to see you again."

I was tired when Rick left. The session had been a contest, a struggle, and as I thought about it, I never explicitly addressed the paradox of his having made such an effort to see me yet resisting almost everything I offered him. All I can do in one session is to be real, to leap into the patient's life, to offer observations in the hope that he'll be able to open doors and explore some new parts of himself in his ongoing therapy. I expected to hear from him, but there was no word for a long time.

Then four months later, an email arrived indicating that Rick's therapy had indeed been catalyzed but in an unexpected way.

Hi, Dr. Y.

I'm better. You did help me and it's time to thank you. Since I returned, my therapist has focused full-bore on my competitiveness and why I couldn't (or wouldn't) admit to you that you had some good insights during our session. She's right, and I've been reluctant to acknowledge it. So, here's something I want to confess. When you said that I regarded Fairlawn Oaks as a prison, you were really right on. And I knew it even then when I was with you but I just refused to admit it. Remember my telling you how fascinated I was by that song?

Well, what I could have shared with you, and didn't, was that I sang you the lyrics of the second stanza of "Don't Fence Me In." I didn't mention the lines of the first stanza. Here they are:

Wildcat Kelly, lookin' mighty pale
Was standing by the sheriff's side
And when that sheriff said, "I'm sending you to jail,"
Wildcat raised his head and cried
Oh, give me land, lots of land under starry skies above
Don't fence me in . . .

—Thanks, Rick

~ 6 ~

Show Some Class for Your Kids

Because I could not stop for Death,
He kindly stopped for me.

These opening lines of an Emily Dickinson poem came to mind when a phone call informed me that Astrid had died from a ruptured aneurism. Astrid, dead? Impossible. An unstoppable life force, Astrid had shaken off one crisis and tragedy after another and kept on walking. Such boundless, crackling energy. And now forever quiescent? No, I couldn't steady that thought in my mind.

Astrid was a therapist for whom I had served as both a supervisor and a therapist for more than ten years, and we had grown close. When an email from her family announced a 'life celebration' for Astrid to be held two weeks later at a local community center, I immediately accepted. On the designated day I dressed in a suit and tie—very rare for me as a committed

Californian—and showed up promptly at noon. Along with two hundred other guests, I was greeted with champagne and hors d'oeuvres. No flowers. Nothing black. No tears or long faces. No suits and not a necktie in sight, aside from mine. Soon a small child, probably one of Astrid's grandchildren, walked through the crowd with a megaphone in hand and announced, "Please take your seats. Ceremony to begin."

We then viewed a polished, forty-minute video celebrating Astrid's life. It took us seamlessly through images of her life. First, as an infant in her father's arms, she yanked off his spectacles and waved them gleefully. Then, in rapid succession, we saw Astrid's first steps toward her mother's outstretched arms, Astrid playing pin the tail on the donkey, Astrid as an adolescent surfing at sunset beach in Hawaii, Astrid at her graduation from Vassar, Astrid as a bride at her most recent marriage celebration (she had married three times), several shots of Astrid pregnant and radiantly smiling, Astrid playing Frisbee with her children, and then the heartbreaking finale that brought tears to my eyes: Astrid gaily waltzing with her six-year-old grandson the evening before her sudden death. When the film ended, we sat silently in darkness. I was sorry when the lights came on because no one knew what to do. One brave, self-confident soul clapped, and soon most of the audience joined in. I found myself longing for a traditional religious ritual, a very rare state of mind for me. I missed the cozy familiar cadence and orderly sequence of events led by clergy and rabbis. What is one supposed to do at a funeral *manqué* that commences with champagne and hors d'oeuvres and has no place for weeping?

After some hurried discussion among themselves, her three children and five of her grandchildren strode in a cluster to the microphone, and each in turn, showing remarkable poise, shared remembrances of Astrid. Each was well prepared and well spoken, but I was most fascinated by an eight-year-old granddaughter who described how Grandma Astrid used to invite them to play by creeping silently up behind them and shaking a box of jigsaw puzzle or Scrabble pieces.

Since this was a life celebration and not a funeral, I was not surprised that there was no mention of her fourth child, Julian, who had been killed by a lightning bolt on a golf course when he was sixteen. But Astrid and I had devoted more than a full year of therapy to dealing with his death.

Next, many of Astrid's friends spontaneously rose to take the microphone and share their memories. After two hours, quiet reigned for a few moments, and I expected someone to signal the end of the event. Instead, to my surprise, Astrid's third and last husband, Wally, rose to address the celebrant-mourners. I was astonished at his composure; I tried to imagine speaking at such an occasion only weeks after my wife's death and knew I would not be up to it. I would not be able to raise my head to the world. I examined Wally closely. For years I had heard Astrid's version of him and was now faced with the odd task of superimposing the flesh-and-blood Wally on the image of him Astrid had given me. Every single time I have encountered a patient's spouse, I have been surprised. Almost without fail I exclaim to myself, *Can this possibly be the same person I've heard about for so many hours?*

To my surprise, Wally was a stately man and much taller, more handsome, and more graceful than I had expected. And far more present. Astrid had often portrayed him as absent, as a man who, even into his seventies, was wedded to his hedge fund and to his office that he always entered at six am to prepare for the opening bell of the stock market. Absent on weekends also, either sailing or fixing his twenty-seven-foot sloop. Astrid told me she had never set foot on it. I remembered our chuckling together when she told me she got seasick whenever she saw a boat, and I responded that I get seasick even looking at a picture of a boat.

"Thank you all for coming to say goodbye to our Astrid," Wally began. "I know there are a lot of her shrink colleagues here, and as you all know, she never tired of teaching. So I'm sure she'd have appreciated my passing on to you a bit of her legacy, her top secret weapon against anxiety: egg salad sandwiches!"

I cringed. *Oh no. Don't do this, Wally. Dear Astrid dead only ten days and you inflict a Jay Leno imitation on us.*

"When Astrid was a child," Wally continued unabashed, "and upset about anything—school, argument with friends, boyfriend trouble, you name it—her mother always soothed her with an egg salad sandwich. Just chopped eggs, mayo, celery, and a bit of pimento on toasted white bread. No lettuce. Astrid called it her Valium and claimed it had four and a half times the potency of chicken soup. Whenever I came home late in the evening and walked from the garage through the kitchen, I always took a look at the sink, and if I spotted eggshells there, I braced myself for the worst."

I looked around. Smiling faces! Everyone except me was en-gaged by Wally's attempts at humor. For a moment I felt very alone, as though I were the only one who seemed to be taking this seriously. Then I reminded myself that I was not the outsid-er—I was the *insider*, the one who really knew Astrid.

Throughout the event, I had vacillated in my feelings. At first, as the speakers described their special contact and their stories about Astrid, I had felt smug about my privileged place in her life. After all, wasn't I the one who had the inside truth, the one who knew the *real* Astrid, the authentic Astrid? But as time passed and I listened to speaker after speaker, I wavered. Perhaps my belief in a privileged place in her life was illusory. Yes, she and I had shared that special hour each week for so many years. And I had access to the real stuff—special knowl-edge of her fears and passions and inner conversations and fantasies and dreams. But was that more real, more true, more privileged than knowing what made her smile? Which folks she liked most? What she liked to eat, her favorite movies, books, shops, yoga poses, music, clouds, magazines, games, snacks, and TV series? The in-jokes with husband and friends, the sexual secrets known only to lovers? I especially wondered if I knew her better than that grandchild who had heard her footsteps as she crept up behind the sofa shaking pieces of a Scrabble game or jigsaw puzzle? Yes, I think it was that grandchild who put me in my place, who made it clear that, though I knew some parts, there was so much of Astrid I never knew.

I had first met Astrid over ten years earlier, when she asked me to supervise her work with several patients. She was fifty, and though she had been in practice for many years, she always sought to sharpen her skills. She was a delightful student: savvy, empathic, intelligent. For the next two years we met for an hour every other week. The supervision was a pleasure. Rarely had I known a student with such wonderful clinical instincts. But toward the end of our second year, things changed between us when she began to discuss her work with one of her patients, a young man named Roy who was a disorganized alcoholic with whom she became uncharacteristically over-involved. She gave him her home phone and took calls from him at all hours of the day or night; obsessed about him frequently during the day, even while seeing other patients; and allowed him to run up a large bill of several thousand dollars that he would obviously never pay. Once Astrid started discussing Roy, she moved from being student to patient. When it is evident that the student has strong and irrational feelings toward a patient ("counter-transference" in the professional jargon), the supervision often must change form.

There was no mystery about the source of her powerful feelings toward Roy: Astrid had a brother, Martin, six years older than she. He had been her savior during and after their mother's death from breast cancer, when Astrid was an adolescent. Martin had protected Astrid from their abusive father, and she remembered the car ride home from their mother's funeral when he put his arm around her, leaned over, and whispered in her ear, "For the rest of your life, Astrid, count on me. I'll be there for you." Martin kept his word until he enlisted in the Marines and served in the 1991 Persian Gulf War, from which he returned with Gulf War Syndrome and multi-drug addiction. Though she did her best to be there for him, she was no match for heroin and could not protect him from a fatal overdose in 2005. Astrid never forgave herself for not saving Martin. Her over-involvement with young Roy was only the latest embodiment of her reliving her attempt to save her brother.

Two years after Martin's death, the lightning bolt that struck her sixteen-year-old son once more shattered the illusion that she could protect either others or herself. Grief after the death of a child is the harshest grief of all. It is, in the words of Yeats, "tragedy wrought to its uttermost," and often there is no outlet beyond tears. Astrid's tears flowed without cease during our twice-weekly sessions throughout the next year. Gradually she rebounded, once in a while even displaying her infectious joie de vivre, and we moved back to a once-weekly schedule, then to a format where we moved back and forth between supervision and therapy. Finally Astrid regained so much of her tranquility that I raised the question of termination, but we never really ended: she took solace in my presence and called every few weeks for a supervisory session.

Then, a year ago, Astrid left a phone message on a weekend evening telling me that she had fallen from her bicycle earlier in the day, suffering only minor injury, but that now her bruises were growing in size at an alarming rate and she was feeling a bit confused. She couldn't reach her internist and asked me whether she should go to the emergency room. I called back and told her that these problems definitely warranted a trip to the ER.

Not hearing back from her during the next few days, I left a couple of phone messages inquiring about the ER visit and received a call from her son, who told me his mother was unable to take calls: she was critically ill in the intensive care unit with a diagnosis of autoimmune liver disease. I knew nothing about this disease. It had not been described when I attended medical school fifty years ago, but a quick search of the medical literature informed me that this was a serious, often lethal ailment for which a liver transplant offered the best chance of survival. Two weeks later I received a call from her son informing me that his mother's condition had deteriorated precipitously; she had severe jaundice and was in acute liver failure. A few days later he called back with great news: the hospital had miraculously located a liver, she had had the transplant, and she was now in serious but stable condition.

Three weeks later I had a brief phone discussion with Astrid, who told me she was getting stronger and was shortly to be released. I visited her at home for a couple of sessions, and soon Astrid was strong enough to travel to my office. "To hell and back," she told me. "The most awful, frightening, anguished time in my life—and as you know, I've had quite a few. For days in the hospital I couldn't stop trembling, couldn't stop weeping. I was certain I was going to die. I couldn't talk to you . . . couldn't talk to anyone. And then, suddenly, I turned a corner."

"How did you do it? Was there a specific turning point?"

"Very specific. A conversation with a nurse—a tough-assed, no-nonsense head nurse who had a good heart. It was just before my children were coming to visit. I had been in extremis for days. I was absolutely terrified of dying; I could not stop shivering and sobbing. And then, just before my family entered my room, she leaned over and whispered in my ear, 'Show some class for your kids.' That changed everything."

"Tell me how."

"I'm not sure how. But it was damned powerful. Somehow it just got me outside of myself. Up to then I just couldn't stop being terrified. I was so close to death so many times. I couldn't talk. Couldn't cope, couldn't even pick up the phone to have a session with you. All I did was cry. That statement, 'Show some class for your kids,' jolted me back to thinking of someone other than myself and let me see that I could still do something for my family, that I could set an example for them. That nurse was something. Tough love."

Astrid was discharged from the hospital, gradually resumed her previous life, and soon began seeing her patients again. But her reprise from death was short. One day a few months later, she slumped forward in her hairdresser's chair and died instantly of a ruptured aneurism in her brain. All this passed through my mind as I walked out of the community center with the other celebrants. All that drama, that hard life, that valiant effort: working through her grief for her mother, liberating herself from her father, surviving her brother's death and, most of all, her son's death. She had worked through so many knotty situations with her own patients and in her own therapy work with me. She had survived her liver disease by virtue of a liver transplant from a young man killed in a motorcycle accident. And, then, all of this remarkable drama extinguished in an instant by a single small artery exploding in her brain. Everything gone in one moment: her extraordinary universe of self; that lush, layered trove of sense data; her teeming memories of a life-time; all that pain, that courage, that struggle and transcendence; that army of transplant surgeons and nurses; all that terror, that wailing, those gutsy recoveries. And for what? For what?

I had left the celebration and was approaching my car about a half block away when a light tap on my shoulder yanked me out of my morose reverie. I turned to see an unfamiliar face: a dour, fiftyish woman with stringy yellow hair, dressed in a plain, frumpy black suit. She hesitated, obviously apprehensive about speaking. "Excuse me, but are you Irvin Yalom?"

I nodded, and she continued, "I thought I recognized you from the photo on the cover of your book."

Wishing to linger in my reverie with Astrid, I felt reluctant to enter into conversation. So I simply smiled and nodded.

"Astrid gave me a copy of your book. I'm Justine Casey. I was one of Astrid's nurses on the surgery ward, and . . . um, I . . . I wonder if you're still taking patients?"

Still taking patients? For many years, at least ten or fifteen, maybe more, no one has ever simply asked me if I were taking patients. It's invariably "Are you *still* taking patients?" One of the endless, unnecessary, and, by now, slightly irritating reminders of my getting on in years. I told her I'd be glad to see her, gave her my card, and asked her to call me for a consultation. As I watched her stride away, I wondered if this was the nurse Astrid had spoken of. Was it she who had whispered in Astrid's ear, "Show some class for your kids"?

When Justine entered my office a few days later, I was struck by how ungenerous nature had been to her. Her proportions were off. Her tight pinched face was too small for her large head, and her roundness was incongruous with her ramrod, head-nurse carriage. She brought to my mind the icy, forbidding Miss Markum, the head nurse on my inpatient ward when I was a resident at Johns Hopkins over a half century ago. I smiled to myself at the words 'my inpatient ward'; in every sense, it was so obviously *Miss Markum's* ward. Ah, the eternal doctor-nurse struggles! Quickly brushing the past from my mind, I sat silently with Justine for a few moments as she swiveled her head slowly, observing objects in my office. Her glance paused at my bookshelf along one wall.

"I see some familiar titles here, Dr. Yalom . . . "

"How would you feel if we went by first names? Irv and Justine?" I almost always say this to patients but rarely so quickly. Perhaps I needed to sweep Miss Markum from my mind.

"Well, all right, but it feels a bit strange—you an eminent professor of psychiatry and I a head nurse."

"Thank you for not saying 'venerable' professor."

She smiled, very briefly. "I'll try but may forget. I'm old school about titles." She glanced again at my bookcase. "I've read several of your books. They were important for me."

"Were those books behind your decision to contact me?"

"Yes, in part. The other part is that our patient, Astrid, spoke so much of how helpful you had been with her. She spoke of you a good bit."

Our patient, I liked that. It might help us bond. "I knew our patient for quite a long time. A good woman. A good therapist, too. But tell me, was there something in these books that particularly spoke to you?"

"Maybe in the book that Astrid gave me, *Staring at the Sun: Overcoming the Terror of Death*. My copy is heavily underlined. I've read it more than once. I'm a surgical nurse and spend all of my time with critically ill oncology and transplant patients. I deal with death every single day at work. Also I liked your novel *The Schopenhauer Cure*. That main character who is dealing with malignant melanoma—I can't get him out of my mind."

"I have a hunch, more than a hunch, that you're already addressing this, but let me ask more directly: Tell me, why have you contacted me? What are you dealing with now?"

Justine exhaled loudly, let her arms hang loosely, and leaned back in her seat. "What am I *not* dealing with? There's a lot going on." She paused. Her anxiety was palpable.

"Try to dive in, Justine. You're safe here."

She seemed startled. Perhaps she still wasn't used to my addressing her as Justine. She looked directly at me. I imagined that few people had ever told her she was safe.

"OK," she inhaled deeply, "here goes. I'll start with the heaviest thing. About a month ago I had a mole removed from my foot, and the path report said it was a malignant melanoma. So you can imagine my interest in your *Schopenhauer Cure* character. Julius, right? I've read the section describing his death repeatedly and cried every time."

"I'm so sorry to hear about the melanoma, Justine. Tell me just what your doc said."

"It was not good, but it could have been worse. The lesion was slightly ulcerated and fairly deep, about four millimeters, but the first lymphatic drainage site, the sentinel node, was clear. You know what I'm talking about? The inguinal nodes? When I talk to psychiatrists I'm never clear about how much of their medicine they remember."

"I admit I've got yawning abysses in my knowledge of much current medicine. But I've worked extensively with oncology patients, so I'm following you so far."

"Good. Well, the lack of node involvement is, of course, encouraging, but the depth of the lesion is not good news. I'm not as bad off as Julius, but I've a good chance of recurrence. The pathologist says perhaps nearly fifty percent. So I've been trying to live with that now."

We sat in silence for a few moments. My heart went out to her. A fifty percent chance of recurrence! And if it did recur, she and I both knew there was no effective treatment available. I tried to imagine being in her shoes and felt myself starting to sweat. "That's so hard, Justine. But often it helps to have someone to share it with."

"Wait, there's more."

"Right. I've tagged your earlier statement: 'What am I *not* dealing with?' What else is happening in your life?"

"My work fills most of my life space, and work is painful. Take Astrid, for example. I took care of her for weeks, got to know her well, really well, and now she's dead. We worked so hard. She was so sick, so close to death; her bilirubin and pro-thrombin time were through the roof; her jaundice was as bad as I've ever seen in a patient; and miraculously a liver transplant became available, and we saved her and brought her back to health. And now, a few months later, suddenly—just like that—she's dead. And she's only one of many, many patients.

It's the tale of *most* of my patients, my cystic fibrosis lung transplants, my advanced ovarian or cervical or pancreatic cancer patients. I get close to them, work my butt off to save them, and for what? Generally they die soon. I'm just their escort through the valley of death. My great dilemma is that if I keep my distance, I'm a bad nurse not doing my job. Yet if I do my job, I get scorched."

"Sounds familiar, Justine. So very familiar. Let me share something with you. The other day, when you first tapped me on the shoulder at Astrid's memorial, I wasn't too responsive because I was lost in a reverie with those same thoughts, those exact thoughts, running through my mind. So much work, my work, Astrid's work, your work, and then, in an instant, she's gone. It's hard to get my mind around it."

"I was hesitant about tapping your shoulder last week. I had a feeling I was interrupting something."

"I'm glad you took the chance. But let's keep going. Is there more going on in the rest of your life we should talk about?"

Justine slowly nodded. "The rest of my life . . . that's the problem. There is not enough of the rest. My life is too small. My husband and I split up over twenty years ago." She took a deep breath. "Now the hardest part. I have one child . . . *had* one child . . . a heroin addict. He's in San Quentin doing ten years for deadly assault, dealing, and burglary."

"When you said '*had* one child,' I first thought you were saying he was dead."

"That's precisely what I meant. He *is* dead to me. I pray I never see him again. I've written him off. Completely. I have no children. I'm all alone."

"A lot of pain there."

"There would be pain if I let myself think about it, but as I say, I've written him off. The pain's been unbearable all these years. He violated me in every way, and in the end he stole everything he could from me, and then some."

"Have you sought any help for any of these things, your feelings about your work, your melanoma, your husband, your son?"

Justine shook her head. "Never. I'm a tough bitch. That's my reputation, and I guess I get off on it. I can take care of myself. Even now with you, let it be noted that I'm not asking for much. Two, maybe three, sessions—just enough to regain my bearings. Besides, I'm still in such credit card debt from my son's stealing I don't think I can afford much more. And if the melanoma wakes up and decides to march, who knows how long I can keep working." She stopped and looked directly at me. "Are you all right with that, really short-term? I want you to level with me. Astrid told me you were not a bullshitter."

"I'm okay with short-term. Let's plan on three sessions, today and two more. If you find you need more in the future, we can renegotiate. And I'll be honest, there's something about short-term that feels comfortable. Your term 'scorched' hits home for me: I was scorched by Astrid's death. Yes, short-term sounds fine to me. I think of it as scorch-free."

"Wow. She's right—you're no bullshitter. I'm not used to that. The shrinks on the ward are always weaseling."

"I will assiduously avoid weaseling. Now let me ask you a question you may not have expected. How are things going for you so far in this session? We're just starting out, I know, but you've laid out a lot of your personal life already, and I have a hunch that's uncommon for you."

"Very uncommon. But you're making it minimally painful. I do open myself up to two good friends, Connie and Jackie, friends from college days. We live in different parts of the country, but we stay in contact by Skype or phone at least once a week. Connie's folks have a great vacation home on Lake Michigan, and we have a reunion every summer."

"And they're close confidants?"

Justine nodded, "Yep, they know almost everything. Even about my son. They're my only confidants."

"Aside from me?"

"Right. But I haven't told them about the melanoma. That I've only shared with you."

"Because?"

"I think you know. Cancer is just too heavy. Unless they're close family, people run the other way."

"Would they run? Connie and Jackie?"

"Hmm, not sure. Probably not."

"Then you don't tell them because? . . ."

"Hey, give a girl a break."

"I'm pushing too hard? Sorry."

"No, no. Don't stop. It's probably good for me. I'm the tough bitch who always does the pushing. It's educational for me to be on the other side. What's more, you're pushing in the right spot. You've got a pretty good nose because my reunion with Connie and Jackie is coming up next month, and the last couple of weeks I've been mulling about telling them. In fact, tell you the truth: my going back and forth about telling them or not is probably the major reason for contacting you."

"Let's dig into it a bit. What do you most fear about telling them?"

"Pity, I guess—pity and withdrawal. My contact with them is the place I feel most real, and I don't want to jeopardize it. I worry about losing them. When I was a kid in New York, my grandmother scraped up the money to send me to camp every summer in the Adirondacks. Most of us went for two months but some for only one month. I remember that toward the end of the first month I withdrew from the ones who were leaving early and spent my time with the ones staying. Not much future in relating to the dying."

"You've taken a chance and told me about the melanoma. Any questions you have for me?"

Justine looked directly at me, incredulously. "Whoa, that's a new twist. I didn't think that shrinks answer questions." She thought for a few moments and then said, "Yeah, I do have one, if you're up to it. Do you pity me?"

"I'm honestly not trying to duck your question, but that word, 'pity,' throws me. You have to be more clear about what you mean by 'pity.'"

"Why do I think you *are* ducking my question? Here, let me put it differently. Exactly what did you feel about me when I told you of the melanoma?"

"Sorrow, compassion, concern—those were my first feelings about you. Then I imagined myself being informed that I had a melanoma, and I felt fear—I could almost feel myself begin to sweat. My problem with your word 'pity' was that it has the connotation of someone 'other' or even 'lesser' than me. I pity a starving dog or an injured kitten. But, Justine, you're not 'other.' You're not different from me. You're facing what all of us must sooner or later confront. I have no specific malady, but my hoary age forces me to think about the end of my life all the time. My hunch is that your good friends are going to respond in a similar fashion. Already I personally cannot imagine deserting you, and I cannot imagine *them* deserting you."

In our second meeting Justine thanked me for my advice. She did tell her two friends about her melanoma, and they responded generously and lovingly. She seemed warmer, thanked me with a fleeting smile, and then turned to the topic of her son. For the rest of the session she related the nightmarish tale of her only child.

"Perhaps I should never have married. I never expected to. I was born clunky and awkward. I was never attractive, had no innate feminine guile and no female mentors. My mother died of cervical cancer when I was nine. I had no siblings and a mostly absent father, a gruff uneducated man, a truck driver who was only home weekends. My paternal grandma, an immigrant from Yugoslavia, raised me. She was an unhappy woman who barely spoke English. Men didn't look at me, and though I had some one-night stands, I never had a good relationship with a man. I probably never would have married if I hadn't gotten pregnant and, with the help of my grandmother, forced the father to marry me. That was about five years after nursing school. Marriage was a mistake: he was a brutish, alcoholic lout who was so abusive to James and me that one day when he was at work I packed my suitcases and left with James, then age three, and moved several hundred miles away to Chicago, where I had been offered a job at Michael Reese Hospital. I never looked back. I never contacted my husband again. I doubt if he searched very hard for us. He probably was relieved we were gone."

"Keep going. Tell me about you and James."

"I did my best for him. I was a nurse forty hours a week and a mother the rest of my time. I had no other life. Zero. And James was a problem every step of the way: problems sleeping, walking, speaking, playing with other children. And major disciplinary problems all the way through his life. I've read a lot now, and I think he was born a sociopath, something deep, inbuilt, genetic, unchangeable about him. Also major learning problems. He just couldn't concentrate, never learned to read well, always in special schools. I suspect today he'd also be diagnosed as severe attention deficit disorder.

Justine went on for much of the hour telling me in detail about James's medical and psychological problems and all the treatments attempted. "We tried lots of meds, including Ritalin, anticonvulsants, and even antipsychotics. Nothing helped. I spent all my money on medical and psychological help. All in vain.

"When he entered adolescence, he hit the recreational drugs big-time and used anything he could find. I sent him to detox centers, rehab ranches, and wilderness retreats. He ran away from each of them. He fought everything. Then, around sixteen or seventeen, he met the hard drugs, especially heroin, and he was gone for good. He stole everything he could from me, including thousands of dollars from my credit cards. He robbed my neighbors and friends, and I finally threw him out and disowned him. The next and last I heard was that he was in San Quentin. That's the story. And I am exhausted telling it." Justine leaned back in her chair and wiped her eyes with a tissue.

After a few moments, she looked up and added, "I've been imagining this whole week telling you this story. I rehearsed this conversation with you, and I imagined your response."

"Which was? . . ."

"I imagined you inquiring about positive memories as a young child, about putting him to bed at night, about warm feelings I had about him or the good times we shared. And my answer to you is that *I cannot remember a single one. I mean it. Not a single one.*"

"You're right. You nailed it: that *is* what I would have asked. And your answer is very heavy, very dark. I'm saddened by what you've told me. Saddened for James but even more saddened for you. Tell me, have you shared all of this with Connie and Jackie?"

"Everything. They've been aboard from the very beginning, when James was born, and followed every step of the way. But it's a different experience here today telling the entire story all at once. I've never done that with anyone. I'm wiped out."

"I feel uneasy asking you more, but it's best to get it all out— like excavating an abscess. Tell me, what are you experiencing right now, here with me?"

"Shame. It's like your coming into my home and seeing nothing but filth and rags." She paused briefly and then asked, "Do you have children?"

"Four. I know what it is to be a parent, and I'm able to get in touch with how unbearably painful this is for you. But still, don't stop. I want you to keep expressing it all."

"I must have been a ghastly mother, but believe me I tried—I did everything in my power. But it is shame. It . . . James . . . that creature in San Quentin . . . however you put it, he is a part of me. He's wrapped in a banner for all to see, saying, 'Made by Justine Casey.'"

"Do you think that others think that?"

Justine sobbed and nodded, "Yes, anybody who knows my story."

"I know your story, and I don't think that. Try to keep talking. What other questions are there for me?"

"Am I ghastly? Am I a horror of a mother? Am I James? Is he me?"

"None of the above. I want you to know I'm on your side, Justine. I'm here to help you. Not once, not for an instant, did such thoughts enter my mind. What I *am* thinking about a lot now is how relentlessly harsh you are on yourself. We've got to stop today, but I'd like to focus some of our final session on the topic of being kinder to yourself."

A week later Justine arrived at my office with a folded sheet of paper in her hand. "I had a dream last night, and I know from reading your work that you pay attention to dreams. This one woke me up about four am. I think it had something to do with you."

"Let's go over it."

She unfolded the paper. "This is just a fragment—I couldn't remember most of it . . . I'm walking along a path and climb through a window into a large, dark room. Somehow that path reminds me of the path to your office, but it's night and I can't see much. Then once I enter the room, I hide behind a very small chair and wait. I'm holding a weapon in my hand. Suddenly I notice that the chair is gone. Someone has removed it, and I am totally visible, totally unprotected. I am scared shitless. That's when I woke up drenched with sweat."

"You have hunches about this dream?"

"I've no clue about how to even start. How do we proceed?"

"Since we have only this last session, we don't have time to explore it in depth, but generally I'd ask you to think about certain parts of the dream and just free-associate. That is, just ruminate out loud; let your thoughts run free. But given our shortage of time, let me pitch in first. What strikes me about the dream is the location. You say it resembles the path to my office. Moreover, it was dreamt the night before our appointment. Any thoughts about that?"

"It *was* your path. I could hear the crackly pebbles just like your walkway. But the window and the very large room: they're not familiar. A big room, maybe a movie set? I don't know where that comes from."

"And then you try to hide but behind a very small chair, which doesn't seem to give you much protection. And then that soon disappears. So you're in my office, and suddenly your hiding place is gone. What's *that* make you think of?"

"I see where you're going. I'm here in this office, maybe it was your office, and my cover is yanked away, and I can't hide, and I get very scared."

"You say your cover was yanked, but you yanked it by your decision to come."

"It was tougher than I thought. I couldn't or didn't hide from you and was bare-breasted."

"Bare-breasted?"

"I didn't mean that . . . " Justine blushed. "What I meant was I got everything off my chest."

Strange slip and probably loaded with meaning, but there was no time to explore it in this last session. I tagged it and put it into storage, in case Justine opted to return for longer therapy, and responded, "Another aspect of the dream is that it is night, you are entering surreptitiously by going through a window, and you hide inside. I wonder if that refers to the unusual way you contacted me. Meeting at Astrid's memorial and making an appointment there is somehow not the same as coming into my office through my front door. And then you make sure it will be for a very few sessions."

"Yes, that's right on: I see your point."

"But I keep thinking about that pistol you're carrying. What hunches do you have about that?"

"I never said anything about a pistol. I said I had a *weapon*."

"Tell me: Do you still see the dream in your mind's eye?"

Justine closed her eyes and seemed to drift off, "Right, it's there. I can see it, but it's a little faded, but I can see that I'm carrying a weapon, and it's definitely not a pistol. I'm carrying something large, huge. It's a bazooka—no, no, it's an atomic bomb." She opened her eyes and shook her head.

"Lot of feeling there. Stay with it; keep going. What about that huge weapon?"

"The dream says I am dangerous."

"Say more about being dangerous."

"Truth is, I *am* dangerous. Venomous. I'm full of anger. Bad, angry thoughts about everyone circle through my mind. That's why I stay away from people. That's why I'm so alone."

We remained silent for a minute or two. The time had come. I hesitated while I formulated what I wanted and needed to say to her. "There's something I've wanted to tell you. I've hesitated until now because of my discomfort about patient confidentiality. It's something Astrid told me during our therapy, and usually I'd never repeat anything told to me by a patient. But this may be so important for you to hear that I can't be silent. Moreover I'm certain Astrid would not have minded my sharing this."

Justine's eyes were riveted on me.

"Astrid told me about a time when she was at her worst, full of terror, certain she was dying, unable to control her sobbing. She was awaiting the arrival of her family when a nurse bent over and whispered in her ear, 'Show some class for your kids.'"

I stopped and glanced at Justine. Her face, her whole body was deathly still, as though frozen in time.

"She gave me no name but only said it was a nurse who was tough but whom she highly respected. Was it you, Justine? Did *you* say that to her?"

"Yes, I said that to her."

"Astrid told me that those words, your words, were 'transformative.' She called it the turning point in her ordeal. She said those were the most helpful words she had ever heard."

"Why? How?"

"She said it immediately, miraculously, brought her out of herself, that it made her think of others, that it gave her a sense of meaning, that it told her that, even if she were dying, she *still* had something to offer her family—she could model how to face death. You gave her a priceless gift."

Justine sat silently for a long time until she said, "Good God. This is the cruelest joke." She looked away staring out of my office window, and she spoke as though in a trance. "The cruelest of jokes. You see, I didn't *whisper* that into Astrid's ears. I *hissed* it. Yes, *hissed* it. Astrid had everything—a room full of beautiful vases and flowers, a golf-ball-sized diamond ring . . . beautiful grandchildren, big family and friends gathered around her. I'd have given anything to have had her life—even *with* her disease. She held court in her powder blue cashmere robe for an endless stream of beautiful visitors and friends. Her husband told me about his goddamn yacht a hundred times, and her therapist and chum was the important Dr. Yalom with his signed books spread all around her bedside, and yet, despite all that, all she could do was whimper and sob, day after day. She was pitiful. I was spiteful, viciously envious, and totally exasperated by her."

"And yet, despite all that, *you* were the one who brought such great comfort to her. 'Transformative,' she said. You changed her life. What do you do with that knowledge?"

Justine sat silently, slowly shaking her bowed head.

I glanced at the clock. "We're running out of time, and I'm struggling to find closure. Despite all your self-accusations, *the better part of you found the right words to say.* In the end *it is deeds not thoughts that really count.* Let's do a thought experiment, Justine."

She raised her head to stare at me.

"Imagine," I continued, "right here in my office, a row of people you've helped, maybe even transformed. The line starts here"—I pointed to a spot near my chair—"and imagine all the people who are grateful to you, people dead or alive. Can you see folks you remember? Please try hard."

Justine silently nodded.

"I can imagine," I suggested, "a very long line winding out of the office and down the street. Right?"

"Yes," Justine said softly, "I can see them. A few of them back from Michael Reese Hospital days. I see both the living and the dead, the recovering and the moribund. I see Astrid standing there near the head of the line, and yes, it *does* stretch far—all the way into the distance—as far as I can see." A long pause and then, "Thank you, this helps. But there's a lot left. The anger isn't quelled. The vicious thoughts are there on all sides, lying in wait."

"Those thoughts are old, archaic, going back to your early rough, hapless days. And you've come by your anger honestly. Of course, much of your anger and guilt is still tethered to your son, who is disowned but, as we both know, not forgotten. All these feelings have to be exhumed, examined, and, finally, scattered. It will take time and a guide, but you can do it. I'm certain of it, and if you wish, I'm glad to be the guide."

Justine sat there, tears flowing down her cheeks, no longer forbidding, no longer resembling Miss Markum from olden days but softer now, almost winsome, almost huggable. She raised her chin, "You mean that? What about your comment about being scorched?"

"Not doing what's right is worse than being scorched. And what's more, you're worth it. Call me whenever you're ready."

Justine rose and collected her things, and I walked with her to the door. As she left, she turned back to me for a last look. I saw pain and sadness in her eyes and perhaps pride as well. I hoped she would call.

~ 7 ~

You Must Give Up the Hope for a Better Past

"Iwant this to be different from our last consultation. This time I want a complete overhaul. My sixtieth birthday is approaching, and I want to change my life."

Those were Sally's first words. A handsome, forthright woman, she looked straight into my eyes and held my gaze. She was referring to our previous therapy six years earlier, when she had requested four, and only four, sessions to help deal with her protracted grief following her father's death. Though she had used that time efficiently and explored her stormy relationship with her parents in some depth, I sensed there was much more that needed attention, but Sally had been resolute in her wish for only four sessions.

"I'm not sure how much you remember about me," she continued, "but I've worked forever as a physics technician and that's what I want to change. The truth is that my heart's *never* been in that work. My real calling is writing. I want to be a writer."

"I don't recall your mentioning that before."

"I know. I wasn't ready to talk about it then. Not even to talk to myself about it. Now I am ready. And I've contacted you again because I know you're a writer and I think you can help me find my way to becoming a real writer."

"I'll do my best. Fill me in."

"I've made the decision to put my writing first. I've got enough money to do that now, with my retirement benefits and my husband's job. He's an airline pilot, and even though United has stolen the pilots' pensions—the CEO really needed his hundred-million-dollar salary and bonus—my husband still makes good money, at least for the next five years. And the most important thing is that I must have talent."

"*Must* have talent? Tell me about that."

"I mean I *must* have some talent. I won a literary guild fiction prize for new writers when I was eighteen. Four thousand dollars. And that was forty-two years ago."

"A huge award! Quite an honor!"

"Quite a curse, it turned out."

"How so?"

"I got this notion I could never live up to that honor. I began to feel like a fraud and was afraid to show my work."

"What did you write?"

"What *do* I write, we should say, because I've never stopped writing. A bit of everything—an unending stream of poetry and stories and vignettes."

"And what have you done with all your work? Have you published any of it?"

"Aside from the novella that won me the prize, I've published nothing. Never tried to publish. Not once. But I've still got every piece I ever wrote. Couldn't send anything out and couldn't throw anything out. I put everything in a big box and sealed it with strong tape. Everything I've written since my teens."

A big sealed box containing everything she's ever written! My heart began to race. *Slow down*, I said to myself, for I was slipping into my identity as a writer and felt myself getting too involved. My curiosity was aflame. And my empathy, too. I shuddered as I imagined my entire life's work stored away unseen in a large box. *Don't over-identify*, I told myself. *Nothing good will come of it.* I turned back to Sally.

"What's that like for you?"

"What? Having everything in that box?"

I nodded.

"It's not so bad. Out of sight, out of mind. It worked just fine . . . until now. I can tell you a lot about the blessings of denial. I've always thought your profession lacked a proper appreciation for denial."

"Right! We don't invite denial to our campfire. I confess that I expect my patients to doff their denial and hang it in the cloakroom before entering."

We smiled together. We were a good pair. When had I last uttered "campfire," "doff," and "cloakroom" during a therapy hour? I sensed us settling comfortably into a writerly conversation. *Careful, careful,* I thought. *She has come for help, not conviviality.*

"That box—where do you keep it?"

"Actually there are two boxes. Box number 1, the main guy, is jammed full, taped shut, and stored out of sight, way in the back of my closet. I've jettisoned a lot of things over the years—clothes, photos, books—but not that box. I've carried that box around with me, as a tortoise lugs its shell, from dwelling to dwelling for most of my life. In it is all my work from adolescence until about fifteen years ago. The second box, where I store all my recent work, is open for business under my desk."

"So you've saved your whole life's output of writing and keep it close but out of sight?"

"No, not my entire oeuvre. A good bit from even earlier years met a sad fate."

"How so?"

"It's an odd story. I'm pretty sure I didn't tell you this in our previous therapy. One day when I was about fourteen, my parents and brothers were out, and I began snooping through the dresser drawers in my father's bedroom. That was not unusual for me. I can't recall what I was looking for, but I've always been a hard-core snooper. On this particular day I found two of my poems in a drawer containing my father's sweaters. The paper seemed damp, as though my father's tears had fallen on them. I had never given him my poems, and I was absolutely enraged that he had them. How could he have gotten them? There was only one way: *he* must have snooped through *my* room when I was at school and stolen them."

"And so . . . "

"Well, I couldn't very well confront him with it, could I? That way I'd have to admit I was snooping in *his* closet. So I had only one recourse."

"Which was . . . "

"I burned all the poems I had ever written."

Ouch! It felt like a stab in the heart. I tried to hide it, but she missed nothing.

"You winced when I said that."

"Burning all the poems you had ever written! I'm trying to conjure up a picture of that fourteen-year-old girl striking a match and setting her poems on fire. What a painful, horrendous thought. Such violence toward yourself! Tell me, Sally, do you have any sympathy for that young, fourteen-year-old girl?"

Sally looked touched. She tilted her head back and glanced upward for a few seconds, "Hmm. I've never addressed that particular question before. I'll have to think on it."

"Let's tag it and make sure we return to it later. It's important. For now though, let's talk more about your reasons for coming." I would have greatly preferred to return to that mysterious taped-up box—it drew me in like a nail to a magnet—but Sally's story of burning her work when her father invaded her privacy gave me pause. The situation called for great discretion. She'd get back to that box, I was sure of it, but only on her schedule, only when she was good and ready.

Over the next few months we prepared the ground for her new life. First she had to deal with retirement, a major, often frightening transition that few navigate with equanimity. Though she was fully aware of the many obstacles in her way, she was also a determined, efficient woman who composed a checklist and checked off one item after another.

First she had to come to terms with the irreversibility of her decision. Her particular field of physics moved so quickly that her knowledge base would soon be outdated, and she knew that she would not have the option of changing her mind in the future and reclaiming her job. To make sure that her lab would function without her, she instigated a thoughtful administrative reorganization, insuring a smooth transition.

Next she addressed loneliness. Her husband planned to continue to fly for five more years and was away fifty percent of the time, but she knew she could count on a bevy of friends. And then there was the question of finances. At my suggestion, she and her husband consulted a financial advisor and learned they had sufficient funds for retirement, provided they gave their children less money. They then arranged a meeting with their two sons, who reassured her that they could manage on their own.

The final item on her list—where to write?—was particularly bothersome to Sally, and she fretted about it for weeks. To write well, she required absolute silence, solitude, and restful contact with nature. Eventually she located and rented a nearby loft encircled by the arms of a massive California oak.

And then one day, to my great shock, she entered my office carrying a two-foot-by-two-foot box, a box so heavy that the floor quivered when she set it down between us. We sat in silence looking at it until she extracted a large pair of shears from her purse, kneeled on the floor next to the box, looked at me, and said, "Today's the day, I guess."

I tried to slow things down. Sally's eyes were red, her lips trembled, and her grip on the shears seemed unsteady. "First, let me ask what you're feeling. You look so strained, Sally."

Sitting back on her heels, she replied, "Even before our first session, I knew that this day would come. This is why I came to see you. I've dreaded it, hardly sleeping several nights, especially last night. But I woke up this morning somehow knowing that now was the time."

"What did you imagine happening when you opened it?" I had posed that question in the past, but it had never proved fruitful. On this day, however, she was forthcoming.

"There are a lot of dark chapters in my life, darker episodes than I've conveyed to you, and there are a lot of dark stories in that box, stories that I may have mentioned, but only obliquely, in our therapy. I'm afraid of their power, and I don't want to get sucked back into those days. I'm very frightened of that. Oh yes, as you know, my family looked good from the outside, but inside . . . inside there was so much pain."

"Is there a particular story or poem that you dread meeting again?"

Rising from the floor and setting down her scissors, Sally settled back into her chair. "Yes, one story that I wrote when I was in college haunted me all last night. 'Riding on the Bus' I think it was called, and it was about me at thirteen, a period when I was so unhappy I seriously considered suicide. In the story—a true story—I boarded a bus and rode to the end of the line and then kept riding it back and forth for hours contemplating how to end my life."

"Tell me more about not sleeping last night."

"It was bad. My heart pounded so hard I felt the bed shaking. I was terrified of that particular story and how I sat all day on the bus, thinking of killing myself. I remember being unable to find a reason to continue living. I kept imagining myself opening the box, rummaging around, and then finding that story."

"You were thirteen then, and you've just turned sixty. So that means the bus ride was forty-seven years ago. You're no longer that thirteen-year-old girl. You're all grown up now; you're married to a man you love, mothered two fine sons; you love being alive, and you're here today planning to pursue your real calling. You've come so very far, Sally. And yet you hold onto the idea you'll be sucked back into the past. How—when—did that odd myth take hold?"

"Long ago. That's why I taped the box shut." She picked up the shears again. "Maybe that's why I brought it here to your office."

I raised my eyebrows and gave her my best puzzled look. "How so?"

"Maybe if you're with me, you'll hold me and keep me in *this* world."

"I'm a good holder."

"You promise?"

I nodded.

With that, Sally again kneeled on the floor, methodically cut the tape—doing as little damage as possible to this treasured box she had lived with most of her life—and gradually pried open the lid. Then she sat back in her chair, and we both stared in silence, in awe, at the startled stacks of paper, the dusty literary record of her life. She picked one sheet at random and silently read a poem.

"A little louder, please."

She looked at me in alarm. "I'm not used to sharing this stuff."

"What better time than right now to break a bad habit?"

Her hands trembled as she looked at the page. She cleared her throat a couple of times. "Well, here are the first lines of a poem I don't recall at all. It's dated 1980."

To want words
Is not hunger
But disease
Dis ease
A lack of mountains
Comfort collapsed
Just flat
Landscape
Eating the evening up
Like a train
Across Wyoming
Roaming those thought tracks
My feet made to scale
Like those of fowl that
Pace the low tide shore
Till water or words rise
To level all sign
Of unusual bird
Or strange mind

Tears came to my eyes. I found it hard to find words. "It's a stunning poem, Sally. Stunning. I love it, especially those last two magnificent lines."

Sally took a handful of tissues, lowered her head, and wept for a few minutes. Then, dabbing her eyes with a tissue, she peeked up at me. "Thank you. You can't imagine how much that means." She spent the rest of the session sifting through the ancient pages of her life, occasionally reading passages aloud, and then, as the end of our time approached, sat back in her chair and took two deep breaths.

"Still here in the present with me?" I asked.

"Still rooted in 2012. I'm so glad you're here. Thank you. I couldn't have opened this without you."

I glanced at the clock. We had run past the hour. Sometimes patients catch that glance and conclude that I'm impatient for the hour to end. But often, like today, it was just the opposite. I was hoping we had more time to pursue the path we were treading.

"We're going to have to stop now, but first we should plan how to proceed. For sure I think we should meet tomorrow or the next day."

Sally nodded assent.

"And do you feel comfortable looking through your writing at home? Or would you prefer to leave the box here with me, and we'll continue looking together next time."

As she thought about my question, I added, "I promise not to snoop."

Sally elected to take the box home and to meet again two days later. After she left, I thought about what a privileged profession I had. What an honor to share such pivotal and precious moments! And listening to her read her poetry was such a treat. I'm tone deaf and never appreciate concerts or opera but have always delighted in the spoken word—theater and, above all, poetry readings. And here, today, I am being paid to be present at this extraordinary drama and to listen to exquisite lines of poetry. I felt guilty at enjoying my hour with Sally so much. Of course, I knew it was problematic—without doubt transference was haunting this session, and the hovering image of her father vastly increased the complexities of her sharing her work with me. And there was also the issue of how I, a professional writer, might respond to her artistry. Some therapists decline to read a patient's writing for fear of damaging the relationship. They worry about what they would say if they disliked or couldn't comprehend the writing. I've never fretted over that. I have too much respect for anyone seeking to cultivate creativity. If the writing is not to my liking, I can always find some lines that move me and point those out to the writer. That's always welcome and often helps writers to raise their work. In this instance, no problem whatsoever arose, since Sally was a gifted writer and all I had to do was tell the truth.

For many weeks she read through her work and painstakingly entered everything, every word, into her computer. The task proved to be a treasure trove for the work of therapy, in that she arrived at each session brimming with vivid recollections about her relationships with her parents, siblings, friends, and past lovers. In her early twenties a series of poems, each sounding more pained and more desperate, presaged the collapse of her first marriage. One day she appeared at my office holding a bundle of sixty-six love poems written to Austin, a demon lover with whom she had had a brief passionate affair in her youth. The poems sang of soaring, unending love, but all too soon her relationship with Austin peaked and then ended badly with a foul aftertaste. She had misjudged him and ended up feeling exploited and traumatized. Hence, when she discovered those poems, her first impulse was disgust, and she considered burning them but desisted until she spoke to me. I was horrified at the thought. I never burn anything and have a large folder entitled "Cuts," holding all the material cut from my novels and stories. I told all of this to Sally in my appeal to save the poems from the fire. I stalled for time by asking Sally to read aloud some of the poems about Austin. With quavering voice she read a few passages.

"I think they're lovely," I said.

She began to weep. "But they're fraudulent. And I'm fraudulent too. The few months during which I wrote these was the most glorious time of my life—and yet these poems are rooted in a dung heap." We spent the last fifteen minutes of the session discussing the many great works of art that had unsavory beginnings. I presented arguments, one after the other, pleading for the life of these innocent poems. I told her the transformation of dung into beauty is artistic triumph, and that if it weren't for errant passion, death, despair, and loss, the great bulk of art would never have been born. She eventually acquiesced and ultimately transcribed the sixty-six poems to Austin into her computer. I felt like a hero who had rescued a precious ancient manuscript from the flames.

Much later, when we were reviewing our therapy, I was to learn that this episode was far more than a short subject accompanying the main attraction of unpacking the mysterious sealed box. Because Sally was so ashamed of the affair and her participation in Austin's elaborate bondage rituals, she had never shared this with a living soul in all these decades. Revealing all to me and getting a supportive response had great impact. She felt enormously liberated and, for the first time, asked for and received a hug at the end of the session.

That night she had a dream. "I found a pile of folded laundry by my door that someone, possibly my husband, had placed there. I started to put it back in the washing machine—it might have gathered dust sitting there—but then I decided against it and put the clothes in my dresser." The dream message was all too clear: she had no more dirty laundry to wash.

All the while, as Sally sifted through her stories and poems, and we discussed all the variegated and rich issues contained therein, I anticipated the uncovering of more portentous themes. Where were all those dark works that had caused her to bury her writing for a lifetime? Where, for example, was that dreaded bus story?

And then one day it arrived. She entered my office holding a folder. "Here's the story. Would you please read this?"

I opened the folder. The five-page story was entitled "Riding on the Bus." It was a simply told story of a young girl hugely upset by a fight with her parents and by taunting from cruel classmates. She decides to cut the rest of the school day and, for the first time, seriously considers suicide. It is a freezing winter day, far too cold for the hour's walk home, and yet she has no money to take the bus. Her father's office is nearby, but the previous day he refused to come to her assistance during a heated confrontation with her mother, and she was still too enraged with him to ask for a ride home or for bus money. And so the young girl steps onto the bus and pulls her pockets inside out to indicate she has no money. The bus driver starts to refuse her entry but, seeing how she shivers from the cold, simply nods for her to board. She sits in the back of the bus and weeps softly the entire trip. At the end of the route all the passengers disembark, and the driver turns the engine off. He is about to get off the bus for his ten-minute coffee break when he notices the sobbing young girl and asks why she hasn't gotten off. She tells him she lives at the other end of the route, and he not only lets her stay on the bus but also buys her a Coke and invites her to sit near him by the heater in the front. For the rest of the day the girl and the driver ride back and forth together on the bus.

I looked up from the story. "*This* is the dark story you dreaded so much?"

"No, I never found that story."

"And *this* story?"

"I wrote it yesterday."

I was speechless. We sat in silence for a few minutes until I ventured, "You know what I've been thinking? Remember what I said to you a few weeks ago, when you had come to realize that your parents weren't cruelly withholding love but that they simply didn't have it to give?"

"I remember clear as a bell. That was when you said that I had to give up the hope for a better past. That phrase caught my attention and has been circling in my mind ever since. I didn't like it, but it was helpful. It got me over a tough spot."

"Giving up the hope for a better past is a potent idea. I've uttered it to help many others, and it's also helped me personally. But today, here," I handed her back the story, "you've given it a creative and unexpected twist. You didn't give up the hope for a better past; instead you've written a new past for yourself. Pretty impressive route you've taken."

Sally put the story back into her briefcase, looked up, smiled, and offered one of the loveliest compliments I've ever received: "It's not so hard if you've got a kind bus driver."

~ 8 ~

Get Your Own Damn Fatal Illness: Homage to Ellie

While on a monthlong writing retreat in Hawaii, I was shocked to receive this email from my patient Ellie:

Hello Irv,

I'm sorry I'll have to say goodbye this way, not in person. My symptoms got a lot worse a week or so ago and I decided to do a process of VSED (voluntarily stopping eating and drinking) in order to die faster and with less suffering. I haven't drunk anything for over 72 hours now and should (according to what I have read and been told) start "fading" soon, and die within a couple weeks at most. I've also stopped my chemotherapy. Goodbye Irv.

I'd known from the onset of our work that Ellie would die from her cancer, but, even so, I was stunned by this message.

I closed my computer, put my work aside, and stared at the ocean.

Ellie first entered my life five months earlier, also via email.

Dear Doctor Yalom,

About a year or so ago I attended your radio interview at The Marsh Theater in San Francisco and felt immediately that you would be a great person to consult. I also liked your book "Staring at the Sun." My situation is that I'm 63 years old and have a fatal illness (recurrent ovarian cancer, initially diagnosed about 3 years ago). I'm currently feeling quite well physically, but I'm in the process of going through all the known chemo drugs that keep the disease in check and, as each drug outwears its usefulness, I can feel that endpoint drawing nearer. I feel I could use some help figuring out what's the best way to live under the circumstances. I think, no, I'm certain, that I think too much about dying. I'm not thinking of on-going therapy but perhaps one or two sessions.

I didn't experience Ellie's email as unwelcome or unusual (aside from being well written and fastidiously punctuated). I almost always have one or two terminally ill patients in my practice and have grown confident that I can offer something of value even in a brief consultation. I replied immediately, offering her an appointment a week later, giving my address, and informing her of my fee.

Her first words as she appeared in the doorway of my San Francisco office, perspiring profusely and fanning herself with a folded newspaper, were "Water, please!" She had raced to catch a bus at the corner near her apartment in the Mission district and then climbed two steep blocks to my office at the top of Russian Hill.

Aging and small in stature, about five foot two, apparently inattentive to her appearance, with tangled hair that cried out for brushing, loose, shapeless clothing, and no jewelry or makeup, Ellie struck me as a faded, wistful flower child, a refugee from the sixties. Her lips were pale and cracked, her face showed weariness, perhaps even despair, but her eyes—her wide, brown eyes—gleamed with intensity.

After fetching a glass of ice water and placing it on a small table next to the chair where she would sit, I took my seat across from her. "I know what a climb you've had to get here, so catch your breath, cool off a bit, and then let's begin."

She took no recovery time. "I've read some of your books, and I can hardly believe I'm here in your office. I'm grateful, most grateful, to you for responding so quickly."

"Tell me more of what I should know about you and how I might be helpful."

Ellie chose to begin with her medical history and described at length, in a mechanical tone, the course of her ovarian cancer. When I commented that she almost seemed detached from her own words, she nodded her head and responded, "Sometimes I go on automatic pilot. So many times have I gone over this story. Too many times! But hey, hey," she hastened to add, "I'm cooperating. I know you need to know my medical history. I know you *must* know it. *And yet, still, I don't want you to define me as a cancer patient.*"

"That I shan't do, Ellie. I promise. But, still, fill me in a bit more. Your email states that you've exhausted the usefulness of several chemotherapy drugs. What does your oncologist tell you? How sick are you?"

"His words to me a month ago at our last visit were 'We're running out of options.' I know him well. I've studied him a long time. I know his sanitized, coded way of speaking. I knew he was really saying, 'This cancer is eating you alive, Ellie, and I can't stop it.' He's tried all the new drugs, and each one had its day in the sun: each one worked for a while and then weakened and finally grew entirely ineffective. A month ago at our visit, I pressed him hard, really hard, for straight info. He fidgeted a bit. He looked so uncomfortable and so sad, I felt guilty for pressuring him. He's a really good guy. Finally, he replied, 'I'm so sorry, but I don't think we have more than a year.'"

"A hard message to hear, Ellie."

"In one way, yes, very hard. But in another way I almost felt relief. Relief at finally, finally getting a straight message from the medical profession. I knew it was coming. He didn't tell me anything I didn't know. After all, I heard him say two years ago that it was highly unlikely I would survive this cancer. During this time I've had a whole parade of feelings. At first I was appalled by the word 'cancer.' I felt polluted. Terrorized. Ruined. It's hard to remember those times, but I'm a writer by trade and jotted down descriptions of my feelings during that period. I'll gladly email them to you if you'd like."

"I'd very much like to see them." And indeed I meant it. Ellie struck me as uncommonly lucid and articulate. Rarely had I heard a patient discuss mortal issues so forthrightly.

"Gradually," she continued, "much of that terror has lifted, though there are still times I scare myself by imagining what my cancer looks like, and I search the web for hours for pictures of ovaries infested with cancer. I wonder if it's bulging, if it's about to burst open and spew cancer seeds all over my abdomen. Of course I'm just guessing about all this, but one thing I know for sure is that the idea of limited time has changed the way I plan to live."

"How so?"

"So many ways. For one thing, I feel different about money, way different. I don't have much money, but I figure I might as well spend what I have. I've never had much. I've worked most of my life at low-paying jobs as a science writer and editor . . . "

"Oh, that explains that beautifully written, meticulously punctuated email."

"Yes. God, I abhor what email is doing to language!" Ellie's voice grew more charged. "No one cares about spelling or punctuation or happy, fulfilled sentences. Be careful—I could talk forever about that."

"Sorry, I've gotten you off track. You were speaking of your attitude toward money."

"Right. I've never made much, never focused on it. And having never married nor had children, I see no point in leaving money behind. So, after my last talk with my oncologist, I made a big decision: I'm going to blow my savings and take a trip with a friend to all the places I've always wanted to see in Europe. It's going to be a grand tour, a real first-class splurge." Ellie's face sparkled, and her voice grew enlivened. "I am so looking forward to this. I suppose I'm gambling, making a bet that my doctor is right. He said one year, so I've given myself a bit of a margin and put aside enough money to keep me going for a year and a half, and I am going to blow all the rest on my trip. It'll be a blast."

"And if your doctor's wrong? If you live longer than that?"

"If he is wrong, then, to put it in technical terms, I'm totally fucked." Ellie flashed a big mischievous grin, and I grinned right back.

I got a big kick out of her bet. I've always been a betting man myself, never turning down an offer to bet with my friends, even my children, on baseball or football games, enjoying my few trips to the horse races, and always relishing my ongoing poker game. Moreover, I felt delighted at the thought of Ellie's grand tour.

She described the busyness in her mind. "I have some good days, but too often I picture myself in the future: weak, declining, close to death. I often ask myself, 'Will I crave to have people with me at the end? Will I be afraid to be alone? Will I be a burden to others?' Sometimes I imagine behaving like a dying animal and crawling off into a cave to hide from the world. I live alone. I don't like it, and sometimes I think of doing what I used to do, renting a huge place and getting a whole new set of roommates. But how could I manage that now? Imagine advertising for roommates and saying, 'Oh, and by the way, I'll be dying soon of cancer.' So those are the bad days. But, as I say, there are good days too."

"And the good-day thoughts?"

"I check into myself often. I ask, 'How're you doing, Ellie?' I tell myself the story of myself. I remind myself of helpful perspectives, for example, that I'm alive now, that I'm happy to be involved in life, not paralyzed with worries as I was a year ago. But in the background there is growing darkness. I'm always aware that I have a fatal condition."

"Always there?"

"Always there . . . it's the static that never goes away. When I meet a friend who is pregnant, I start calculating whether I will still be alive when the baby is born. The chemo I take makes me feel awful. I keep asking myself, 'Is it worth it?' I often play with the thought of decreasing my dose, of trying to fine-tune it so that I could feel better and live a couple of months less, say nine or ten months of good life rather than a year of bad life. And then, there's something else: sometimes I think I grieve for the life I haven't had. I guess I have regrets."

That statement instantly caught my attention. An exploration of regrets almost always takes the discussion deeper.

"What kind of regrets, Ellie?"

"I guess regrets for not being bold enough."

"Bold? How?"

She sighed and thought for a minute. "I'm too introverted; I've stayed hidden too much, never married, never stood up for myself at work, never asked for more money. Never spoke out."

I considered pursuing the longing and sadness in her voice but instead chose a bolder path. "Ellie, this may seem like a strange question, but let me ask you, Have you been bold enough in this conversation with me today?"

I was taking a chance. Though Ellie was being honest and sharing difficult things, somehow, for reasons I couldn't quite put my finger on, I felt a certain distance between us. Perhaps it was my fault, but somehow we weren't fully engaged, and I wanted to remedy that. Many individuals with a fatal illness feel isolated and think that others hold them at arm's length, and I wanted to make certain that wasn't happening here. Redirecting the flow of the interview into the here and now almost always enlivens therapy by tightening the connection between therapist and patient.

Ellie was startled by my question. Whispering aloud to herself two or three times, 'Have I been bold enough here?' she closed her eyes, thought for a few seconds, and then suddenly opened them, turned to look directly into my eyes, and declared firmly, "No. Certainly not."

"And if you *were* to be bold here, what would you say to me?"

"I'd say, 'Why are you charging me so much? Why do you need so much money?'"

I was flabbergasted. As I often do, I had deliberately phrased my words in the conditional tense to encourage boldness, but never, not in the farthest realm of my imagination, did I expect such a bold response from this wounded, docile, soft-spoken woman, who seemed overwhelmed with gratitude that I would see her at all.

"Uh . . . uh," I stuttered, "I'm a bit uh, uh . . . flustered. I don't quite know how to answer you." I couldn't think clearly and paused to collect my thoughts. I felt a flush of shame about my fee, especially when I thought of how she was scrimping, taking the bus to my office, scraping money together for her grand tour. In dilemmas like this I eventually turn to my own personal mantra, *tell the truth, tell the truth, tell the truth* (at least insofar as I deem it helpful to my patient). After a short time I collected myself.

"Well, Ellie, obviously I'm uncomfortable at your saying this to me, but first I want you to know—*and I really mean this*—I'm absolutely thrilled at your boldness just now. And the reason I'm flustered is because you've touched on one of my own personal dilemmas. My immediate reflex was to defend myself and say to you, 'My fee is the going rate for San Francisco psychiatrists,' but I know that's not your point. The fee *is* high, and your implication is right on: *I don't need the money.* So you're confronting me with my own personal ambivalence about money. I can't work this through right now, but I do know one thing for sure: I want to make a proposal. I'd like to cut your fee in half. Is that okay? Will that be affordable?"

Ellie showed a flash of surprise but then simply nodded appreciatively and then quickly changed the subject by discussing her daily routine and how she often makes things harder for herself by thinking she has to do something very substantial with her limited time, like writing her memoirs or starting a blog. I agreed that this represented an area for work if she were to pursue therapy, but it seemed apparent to me that she had jumped too quickly away from our discussion about fees. For a moment I considered suggesting that we reexamine our feelings about what had just happened, but then I thought, *Slow down—you're asking too much of her. This is only a first session.*

Ellie looked at the clock on the table between our chairs. Our hour was nearly up. She hurriedly offered me some compliments. "It's been good to talk with you today. You really do listen. You do receive me. I feel comfortable with you."

"Can you say what I've done that's made it comfortable for you today?"

Ellie paused for a few seconds, stared at the ceiling, and then ventured, "Maybe it's because of your age. I've often found it easier to talk about dying with an old person. Maybe it's because I sense that old persons have thought about their own death."

Her would-be compliment ruffled me. It was appropriate to talk about her death, but had I signed on to talk about *mine*? I decided to air my feelings. After all, if I weren't going to be honest, how could I expect it of her? I chose my words carefully.

"I know you mean that well, Ellie, and what you say is entirely, indisputably true: I *am* old, quite old, and I *have* thought much about my death. But still I'm a bit rattled by your comment. How to put it?" I thought for a few seconds and continued, "You know what it is? I think it's because *I just don't want to be defined as an old person.* . . . Yes, yes, I'm sure that's it, and there's a parallel here with what you said earlier. This helps me understand exactly what you meant about not wanting to be defined as a cancer patient."

As the hour ended, she asked if we could meet for a second session. It turned out that Fridays, the day I was always in San Francisco, were often not good for Ellie because of her chemotherapy schedule. Nor did she have transportation to meet me in my Palo Alto office, thirty-five miles away. When I offered to refer her to another therapist in San Francisco, she demurred: "I've gotten much from this hour. I feel enlivened, as though I've been reacquainted with living. I know that in my email I asked for only one or two meetings. But now . . . " She stopped, took a deep breath, collected her thoughts, turned to me, and said, "Now I want to ask you something big. I don't want to put you on the spot. I know that you may not be able, or willing, to do this, and I know our schedules don't fit well, and we can't meet every week." She drew a deep breath. "But I wonder if you'd be willing to meet with me until I die?"

Willing to meet with me until I die? What a question! I've never had anyone pose that to me so . . . so boldly. I felt honored by her invitation and quickly gave assent.

In our second session Ellie entered with a stack of old family photos and the agenda of filling me in completely about her family. Rummaging in the distant past, I was sure, was not the best direction for us to take, and I wondered if Ellie, trying to please me, had mistakenly believed that I wanted her to provide an extensive family history. While I searched for a tactful way of saying this, she commenced to speak with much feeling of her deep love for her sister and brothers. Her eyes grew moist, and when I inquired about her tears, she began to sob about the unbearable pain of never seeing them again. Then, when she regained her composure, she said, "Maybe the Buddhists had it right when they said, 'no attachments, no suffering.'"

Propelled to say something helpful, I clumsily fumbled about trying to make a distinction between "love" and "attachment." That went absolutely nowhere. Then I commented on the richness and fulfillment that flowed from her family relationships, and she gently let me know that such reminders were unnecessary, for she already fully appreciated her loving family and was much comforted by the thought that when she needed them at the time of dying, her sister and brothers would all be there for her.

This sequence of events reminded me of an important axiom of psychotherapy that I have learned (and forgotten) so many times from so many patients: *the most valuable thing I have to offer is my sheer presence. Just be with her,* I thought. *Stop trying to think of something wise and clever to say. Let go of the search for some dynamite interpretation that will make all the difference. Your job is simply to offer her your full presence. Trust her to find the things she needs from the session.*

A bit later, Ellie spoke of her strong desire to find some income-producing work. As she described the details of her life, I grew more aware of her truly marginal economic status. She rented a small, one-bedroom apartment in one of San Francisco's most inexpensive areas and adhered to a frugal budget, refusing even the luxury of a taxi to visit my hilltop office. Too ill to hold a paying position for the last two years, she now earned only a few dollars from babysitting and minor editing for a friend. I realized that even my greatly reduced fee was a significant burden and threatened her plan of the grand tour she yearned for. I was rooting for her to take that trip, and I knew that she would be far more likely to afford the splurge if I saw her pro bono, but I sensed her pride would not permit her to accept paying no fee at all. Then an idea occurred to me that might make Ellie more comfortable.

Forty years earlier I had seen a very shy patient, also a writer and also unable to pay for therapy. I had suggested an experimental format in which she would write a summary after each session in lieu of payment, and I would do the same, and every few weeks we would read each other's summaries. I had originally considered that exercise only as a learning tool for both of us—I wanted her to learn to be more honest in her comments about our relationship, and I personally wanted to free myself up as a writer. But the resulting summaries proved to be of such significant value in teaching student therapists, that the patient and I jointly published them as a book (*Every Day Gets a Little Closer*). I told Ellie about this project and proposed that she and I try to rerun this experiment. Given this would not be long-term therapy, I suggested that we both write a summary of each session and email it to the other before the next meeting. Ellie was delighted with this idea, and we agreed to commence immediately.

In her first summary, Ellie reflected on the problems of speaking to others about her illness:

> It's a relief to talk to Irv because he has really faced the question of his own death. It's often pretty hard to speak to others about my cancer. I have a number of pet peeves. Many folks are overly solicitous. They can't do enough for you. There's that Kaiser nurse who keeps asking "Isn't there someone who can drive you here?" And some people are too prying. I think they are voyeuristic and attempt to satisfy their morbid curiosity about having cancer. I don't like that and have sometimes wanted to say, "Go get your own damn fatal illness."

During our following session I made the mistake of saying that I admired her courage, and that touched off a spirited response in her next summary:

Too many people are overly respectful, braying, 'You're so brave' and Irv fell smack into that trap. After all what's so courageous about having cancer? Once we have it, what choice do we have? But the worst thing of all—and thank God Irv doesn't do this, at least not yet—is all this nonsensical talk about a patient's courageous struggle with cancer that all too often ends in defeat. How many obituaries do you see stating that so-and-so lost their courageous battle with cancer? I hate that! I absolutely hate it! If someone put that in my obituary, I'd come back and kill him!

But Ellie's health soon began to deteriorate rapidly. Her chemotherapy was no longer effective, and she grew fatigued and anorexic, and required several hospitalizations to deal with her ascites—an accumulation of abdominal fluid. It soon became apparent that Ellie's dream of the grand tour was not to be, and neither she nor I spoke of it again. And neither would there be a book of our post-session summaries. We ended up meeting for only six sessions, and our summaries were stilted and uninspired. Though hers had a bit of sparkle, her fatigue showed through, and her summaries were burdened with repetitive expressions of gratitude to me for seeing her without a fee. My summaries were cautious and superficial because it was so apparent that Ellie had little energy for engagement. She was obviously dying, and I felt it inappropriate to comment on nuances of our relationship. And so we missed one another and never experienced the authentic encounter I had originally sought.

Moreover, during this period I was entirely consumed with the task of finishing a novel (*The Spinoza Problem*); I departed on a long-planned one-month retreat during which I put all else out of mind and worked nonstop on my final pages until the day I was jolted by Ellie's email letting me know she had stopped all eating and drinking and soon would be dead. I felt both shocked and guilty. Shocked because, even though I knew she was terminally ill, I evidently compartmentalized the knowledge that she was so close to death so as to have all my energy available for writing. And guilty because I knew I could have offered her more of myself. I could have paid home visits when she was too ill to travel, and I could have engaged her more fully in the sessions and in the summaries I sent to her.

Why had we not connected more fully? My first answer to that question was that Ellie simply lacked the ability for deep relationships. After all, she had never married nor maintained a deep and lengthy love connection with any partner. She had moved many times and had had a great number of roommates but few truly intimate friendships. But I failed to convince myself: I knew this wasn't the whole story. I knew that for some reason I had withheld myself from her. Truly shaken by her email, I felt compelled to put my novel on hold for a while and devote myself to Ellie by rereading, meticulously, all our summaries and correspondence. It was an eye-opening experience—so many of her statements staggered me with their great power and wisdom. Again and again I checked the dates of her emails. Had I *really* read these messages before? How could that be? Why did these strikingly poignant words seem unfamiliar, as though I were seeing them for the first time?

I decided to collect Ellie's wisest and most powerful words and write this remembrance of her. I phoned Ellie and told her what I wanted to do and asked her permission. She was pleased and had only one request: that I use her real name rather than a pseudonym.

As I pored over her summaries, I was surprised at how often Ellie wrote about her deep sense of connection with me. Several times she wrote that she spoke more openly to me than to anyone else in the world. To take one example from her fourth summary:

> I hate having to explain my situation to people who are novices to dying. Irv puts me at ease and he's not afraid to go into the darkness with me. I can't speak this way to others. It's hard work, too hard, explaining to them that my cancer is incurable. People can't help asking, "How long will you be on chemo?" which is an upsetting question. Don't they get it? Don't they get that my illness is *not* going to go away? I need people who can look straight into my eyes. Irv is good at that. He doesn't look away.

These and a great many similar comments persuaded me that, despite my sense that I had failed to connect with her, I *had* offered her something precious by my willingness to accompany her into the darkness and not flinching when she discussed her death. The more I read, the more I wondered how I was able to do that.

I do my best thinking on my bicycle, so I took a long ride along the southern Kauai coast pondering that question. For sure it was not because I had entirely overcome my own fear of death. That had been a work in progress, an ongoing project, for a very long time.

Forty years ago, when I first began working with patients with terminal cancer, I was buffeted by storms of death anxiety and frequent nightmares. At that time, seeking solace, I sifted through memories of my personal psychotherapy, a seven-hundred-hour personal psychoanalysis during my residency in psychiatry, and was stunned to realize that *not once in those seven hundred hours did the topic of death arise*. Incredible! My ultimate perishing—the most terrifying fact of my life—had never surfaced, never once spoken of, in that long personal analysis. (Perhaps my analyst, at that time in her late seventies, was protecting herself from her own death anxiety.) I realized that, if I were going to work with terminally ill patients, I needed to do some personal work on my own mortal fears, and I reentered therapy with a psychologist, Rollo May, whose writings suggested a keen sensibility to existential issues.

I can't pinpoint exactly how my therapy with him helped, but I do know that I wrestled with the fact of my death again and again in our work. Rollo was older than I, and looking back on our meetings, I am certain that I often made him anxious. But, to his credit, he never backed away and, instead, consistently pressed me to go ever deeper. Perhaps it was simply the process of opening closed doors and examining and embracing every aspect of my existential situation in the presence of a gentle and sensitive guide that made the difference. Gradually, over the course of several months, my death anxiety diminished, and I grew more comfortable in my work with terminally ill patients.

This life experience made it possible for me to be so present with Ellie, and there is no question that she was appreciative of my honesty. Denial was the enemy, and she voiced impatience with any form of it. In one of her summaries she wrote:

Other people, even others who also have cancer, tell me "You're going to live 30 years." They tell themselves, "I'm not going to die of this." Even Nancy in my support group, so wise and clear-sighted, e-mailed yesterday "All we can hope for is to hang on long enough until better treatments are developed."

But this isn't what I want to hear. This is a safety net with an enormous hole right in the middle. Whether I will live a long time or a short time, I'm alive now, at this moment. What I want is to know that there are other things to hope for besides length of life. What I want to know is that it isn't necessary to turn away from thoughts of suffering or death but neither is it necessary to give these thoughts too much time and space. What I want is to be intimate with the knowledge that life is temporary. And then, in the light (or shadow) of that knowledge, to know how to live. How to live now. Here's the thing I've learned about cancer—it shows you mortal illness and then spits you back, back to the world, to your life, to all its pleasure and sweetness, which you feel now so much more than ever. And you know that something has been given and something has been taken away.

"Something has been given and something taken away." I knew what Ellie meant. It was a simple yet complex thought—a thought that must be unpacked slowly. What has been given is a new perspective on living life, and what has been taken away is the illusion of limitless life and the belief in a personal specialness exempting us from natural law.

Ellie jousted with death using an arsenal of denial-free ideas—ideas so effective she compared them to cancer drugs:

I'm alive now and that's what matters.
Life is temporary—always, for everyone.
My work is to live until I die.
My work is to make peace with my body and to love it, whole and entire, so that, from that stable core, I can reach out with strength and generosity.

Each of these ideas had a peculiar life cycle. As she put it:

After a while each one stops working. It loses its power. Ideas are just like the cancer drugs. Except that the ideas are more resilient—they wear out, lay low for some time, as though they are taking a rest, and then come back revitalized, and also better and stronger new ones keep coming.

Often, especially early in the course of her illness, Ellie was plagued by envy of the living and healthy. She knew these mean-spirited sentiments were unhealthy to her mind and body and struggled to overcome them. The very last time I saw Ellie she told me something remarkable: "Now no more envy. It is gone. In fact, I'm able to feel generous. Maybe I can be a kind of pioneer of dying for my friends and siblings. It sounds weird, maybe Pollyannaish, but it sustains me and is a thought that doesn't fade like the others."

A *pioneer of dying*—what an extraordinary phrase! This took me back forty years, to the first time I encountered this idea in my work as a therapist. In my first group of patients with cancer, I tried hard, week after week, to comfort a gravely ill woman. I've forgotten her name, but I remember her essence and still, with great clarity, can see her despondent, deeply lined face and her sad, downcast grey eyes. One day she startled all of us in the group when she arrived looking bright and revitalized. She announced: "I've made a big decision this week. I've decided to be a model for my children—a model of how to die!" And indeed, until she died, she modeled grace and dignity, not only for her children but also for the group members and for everyone who came in contact with her. The idea of modeling how to die permits one to imbue life with meaning until the very last moment. Over the years, I passed her insight along to many patients, but Ellie's strong language ("a pioneer of dying") gave it even greater force. As Nietzsche said, "If we have our own 'why' of life, we shall get along with any 'how.'"

When Ellie described positive effects of her illness, I was not surprised, since I had heard many such comments from terminally ill patients. But, still, Ellie's words had unusual power:

For family and friends I'm more of a scarce commodity. And I feel special to myself also. My time feels more valuable. I feel a sense of importance, gravitas, confidence. I think I'm actually less afraid of dying than I was before cancer, but I'm more preoccupied with it. I don't worry about getting old. I don't give myself a hard time about what I'm doing or not doing. I feel like I have not just permission but almost a mandate to enjoy myself. I love the advice I came across on some cancer website: "Enjoy every sandwich."

Throughout all of this, she never lost her droll sense of humor.

On raising the bar.

Never in my life have I heard so often, from so many people, how good I look.

Of course there's the unspoken "considering you have cancer"—but hey, never mind, I'll take it! I give myself the same extra credit, patting myself on the back and think 'wasn't I nice to that grumpy salesperson, considering that I have cancer? Aren't I so wonderfully upbeat, for someone who has cancer?'

I didn't get much done today (or all week, come to that), but after all, I have cancer.

It's nice, but I'm getting spoiled. Time to raise the bar.

Almost all of Ellie's comments on her death were arresting. I reread each one several times. Over and again I wondered how

I could have read them before and yet have so little memory of them.

Childhood Thoughts of Death

Having been one of those exhausting children who can't let a subject drop, I pinned Mom down on the death question when I was four or five. She spoke of heaven but it didn't really help. When I looked at the sky all I saw was sky. I ran and hid behind my father's big leather armchair, the one that was pushed up against a corner. I figured I would just stay there forever and death wouldn't find me.

The Buddhists advise living with death on your left shoulder; sometimes I feel like it's sitting on both shoulders and in fact has climbed right inside my body. Which of course is exactly where it has always been.

No, these lines were too strong to have been forgotten. The truth is *I hadn't truly let them into me the first time*. I marveled at the power of denial, *my* denial. So now I read Ellie's words yet again, but this time with eyes and heart wide open. This time, the power of her words took my breath away:

My work is to love my body, all of it. Whole and entire. The whole aging mortal troublesome failing miraculous intricate breathing doomed cancerous warm mortifying unreliable hard-working imperfect beautiful appalling living struggling tender frightened frightening living dying living breathing temporary wondrous mystifying afflicted mortally-ill assemblage of the atoms of the universe that

is my self, is me, for this space of time. This body that is
screwing up. That is growing terrible and dangerous tumors.
That is failing to turn them back, destroy them, dissolve
them, annihilate them. This body that is failing at the one
essential job of life, to stay alive, to stay alive.

Upon first learning that her cancer had spread she had
written:

I stared at a mirror and I saw a human face, vulnerable,
living, beloved, transitory. I didn't examine my skin for
clogged pores or fluff my bangs or form any opinion at all
about my appearance. I looked straight into the eyes that
looked straight back and I thought, oh, poor darling, poor
kid. I think it was the first time I ever saw my face like
that—whole.

These lines brought tears to my eyes. The image of Ellie staring at herself in the mirror and saying, "oh, poor darling, poor
kid," tugged at my heart and also ignited my fears for myself.
Death anxiety never really disappears, especially for those like
me who continue to poke around in their unconscious. Even
after all that work on myself, I continue to have my occasional
three am awakenings during which I replay scenes in which I
learn of my own fatal diagnosis, or lie on my deathbed, or imagine my wife's grief.

Yet Ellie had said I was fully present, fully willing to enter
the darkest places with her. I knew there was truth to that but
wasn't sure how I had managed to do it. Part of an answer came

as I monitored my reactions while rereading these written reflections in one of her summaries.

> Life is temporary—always, for everyone. We always carry our death in our bodies. But to feel it, to feel a particular death with a particular name—that is very different.

As I read these words, I observed myself understanding, nodding, agreeing with Ellie's words, but when I turned up the volume and listened even more closely, I heard a muffled voice from the depths of my mind saying, *Yes, yes, all that is very well, Ellie, but let's be frank, you and I . . . we're not the same. You, poor thing, are the afflicted one, the one with the cancer, and I feel for you, and I'll help in every way I can. But me, I'm healthy—cancer free. Alive. Free from danger.*

Yet Ellie was a perceptive woman. How could she have said repeatedly I was the one person she could really relate to? She said that I looked directly into her eyes without flinching, that I received her and could hold everything she said to me.

What a conundrum. As I poured over her messages, I gradually began to understand. I *did* get close to Ellie. But not *too* close! Not dangerously close. I had falsely blamed her for our lack of intimacy. But she was *not* the problem. She had enormous capacity for intimacy. *I was the problem.* I was protecting myself.

Am I pleased with myself? No, of course not. But perhaps my denial allowed me to do my work. I now believe that all of us who work with the terminally ill must hold these contradictions. We must continually work on ourselves. We must coax ourselves to stay connected and not be too hard on ourselves for being human, all too human.

I look back on my time with Ellie with many regrets. I have regrets for Ellie, regrets that she never lived boldly, that she died young, and that she never took that grand tour. But now, as I look back at my experience with Ellie, I feel regret for myself. In our meetings it was I, not Ellie, who was shortchanged. I missed an extraordinary opportunity for a deeper encounter with a great-souled woman.

~ 9 ~

Three Cries

Though I met her only once for a single consultation many years ago, our hour together remains sharply etched in my mind. A lovely, saddened, well-spoken woman, Helena came to talk about her friend Billy and cried three times during our talk.

Billy, who had died three months earlier, loomed large in her life. Their worlds had been different—he swirling in the Soho gay world, she ensconced in a fifteen-year bourgeois marriage—but they had been lifelong friends, meeting in the second grade and living together during their twenties in a Brooklyn commune. She was poor, he rich; she cautious, he devil-may-care; she awkward, he brimming with savoir faire. He was blond and beautiful and taught her to drive a motorcycle.

"Once," she reminisced with sparkle in her eyes, "we motorcycled for six months throughout South America with nothing but small packs on our back. That trip was the zenith of my life. Billy used to say, 'Let's experience everything; let's leave no regrets; let's use up all there is and leave death nothing to claim.' And then, suddenly, four months ago, brain cancer, and my poor Billy was dead in a few weeks."

But *that* was not when she cried—that happened a few minutes later.

"Last week I reached an important milestone in my life. I passed my state exams and am now a licensed clinical psychologist."

"Congratulations. That *is* a milestone."

"Milestones aren't always good."

"How so?"

"Last weekend my husband took our two sons and their best friends camping, and I spent much of the weekend assimilating this milestone and reviewing my life. I cleaned house, I sorted through closet after closet packed full of useless possessions, and I came upon an old forgotten album of photos of Billy that I hadn't seen for years. I took a deep breath, fixed myself a drink, sat on the floor in a corner, and slowly turned the pages, but this time with starkly different vision—with a therapist's vision. I gazed at my favorite picture of Billy. He was sitting on his cycle, leather jacket unzipped, flashing that miraculous midsummer smile, saluting me with a bottle of beer, and beckoning me to join him. I always loved that photo, but suddenly it dawned on me, for the very first time, that Billy was manic, that Billy had bipolar disorder! I was staggered by the thought. All those treasured adventures, the crazy wild things we did, maybe it all was nothing but . . . "

And it was here that she cried for the first time. She sobbed for several minutes. I prompted her, "Can you finish that sentence, Helena? It all was nothing but? . . ."

Helena continued to weep, shaking her head and apologizing for going through most of my box of Kleenex. Collecting her thoughts, she ignored my question and continued, "It was at that point I phoned you for an appointment. The thought that he was bipolar was bad enough, but later in the day it got even worse as I reread my last emails with Billy. Toward the very end, he wrote me a loving message telling me how much I meant to him, how he treasured my friendship, how he clung to images of me even though chunks of his brain were crumbling away. And then . . . "

At this point Helena broke down and cried for the second time. She reached again for tissues as she sobbed heavily.

"Try to keep talking, Helena."

"And then, as I looked at the email more carefully," she said between sobs, "I realized that his letter had been sent to over a hundred people. That I was just one of a hundred, one hundred and thirteen to be exact."

She continued to cry effusively for several more minutes. As the sobs grew quieter, I said, "And then, Helena?"

"And then I turned to a page in the album I had completely forgotten. Pasted on the page was an invitation to one of the joint wild birthday parties we used to give in Brooklyn. I was born on June 11 and he on June 12. We were born only a few hours apart, and we used to celebrate our birthdays together, and . . . "

Here, for the third time, Helena broke down into tears.

I waited a few moments and then finished the sentence for her, "*We were born only a few hours apart, and now he's dead. Must be a frightening thought.*"

"Yes, yes," Helena nodded vigorously as she sobbed.

I checked my watch. She had asked for a single session, and there were only twenty minutes left. "Helena, let's focus on these last tears first: you and Billy the same age, born within hours of one another. And now he's dead. Tell me more of what you're thinking."

"It's just chance that I'm here and he's dead. It could have been the other way around. I remember one day we went to the horse races. It was my first time. I was surprised that Billy refused to bet, and when I asked about that, he gave a quirky answer. He said that he had already used up his luck by winning the lottery of life—all those millions of other eggs and sperm cells, and he was the one lucky enough to have pulled the winning ticket. He pointed to all the torn losing tickets on the ground and said he owed it to the 'lottery of life' not to throw away his money or to snatch more from others but, instead, to use it to live life to the fullest."

"And did he do that?"

"Oh yes. Oh yes. I never knew anyone so fully alive, so fearless, so exuberant in the sheer act of being alive."

"And," I said, "if that brilliant life spark could be extinguished, then your own life seems precarious."

Helena looked up at me with a bit of surprise in her eyes at my bluntness. "Exactly, exactly." She grabbed another handful of Kleenex.

"So your tears are also for yourself. His death makes your own death more vivid, more real. Is this the first time you've had such an encounter with death?"

"No, no. I think there were many times as a kid when the thought of death thundered down upon me. Every time I attended funerals I had bad sleepless nights thinking about being dead. Also when my oldest son was being born. His first cry hit me hard."

"Why then?"

"It brought home the obvious: that life has a start and then proceeds in linear fashion. I'm just a carrier passing it on to my son, who will pass life along, and then he, too, will face death. I guess it brought home that we're on a schedule, every one of us, and I sure ain't no exception."

"I'll tell you what's on my mind," I said. "It's Billy's statement, 'Leave no regrets.' It seems from what you're saying that your life with Billy was lived fully. Right?"

"Right."

"I see that from the excitement in your eyes as you discuss it. No regrets from that time of life?"

"None at all."

"Well, what about your life *now* with your husband and your sons?"

"Ah, yes. You don't waste time. Different story. I'm not *in* life now. I seem to be postponing it. I'm not really experiencing and savoring life as it happens in the moment. And I'm so weighed down with things: clothes and linen and bedspreads and too many lamps and baseball gloves and golf clubs and tents and sleeping bags."

"Not like your motorcycle trip with Billy—six months of South America with just a small pack on your back."

"Oh, that was heaven. Sheer heaven. Now I'm married to a good man. I do love him, but, oh, I wish I weren't so weighed down. I wish I could go on with just a pack on my back. Too many things. Sometimes I visualize a giant steam shovel breaking through my roof and filling its jaws with our things—giant TVs and DVD players and sofas and dishwashers—and, as it rises to take things away, I see some striped canvas lawn chairs dangling from its teeth."

"And so? Speak more of your regrets about life in the past few years."

"I haven't valued it, haven't lived it as I should have. Perhaps I've hung on too long to the idea that *real life* was back there, with Billy."

"And that belief makes it all the more difficult to come to terms with your *own* death. It's always more painful to think of death when you sense you haven't lived fully."

Helena nodded. I definitely had her full attention now.

"Let's go back to the other two times you cried. You cried when you learned that he had sent a farewell email to over a hundred people. Let's talk more about that."

"I just didn't feel special anymore. We were once so close, so very close."

"You've been seeing a great deal of him?"

"I used to but no, not for the last several years. Not since I moved to Oregon about ten years ago. We've been on opposite coasts, and I saw him about once or twice a year at most."

"So," I mused, "I think of Billy invaded by a brain tumor and perhaps, like so many dying people, feeling isolated and, in desperation, reaching out to touch his entire social network, to contact everyone he knew. That seems understandable and so very human. But by no means, Helena, is his act a comment about his relationship with you."

"Yes, yes, I know that. God, do I know that! I see a lot of couples in my practice, and almost every single day I'm saying to some client or other that every act is not necessarily a message about the relationship."

"Precisely, and it is even *more* unlikely that it is a message about the genuineness of your relationship with Billy so many years ago. Relationships end, but that does not obliterate what they once were. And that brings us to the very first time you wept here, when you spoke of your sudden realization that Billy was manic. Try to imagine what your tears were saying then."

"His mania seems so obvious now. He never stopped. Always at full speed. He never slowed down. *How could I have missed it? Unbelievable.*"

"But let's look at why it shook you up so."

"I think it called into question my whole sense of reality. What I used to consider the peak of my life, the glowing exciting center, the time when I, and he, were most thrillingly alive—*none of that was real*. Now I realize that it was all just the mania talking."

"I can appreciate how destabilized you must feel now, Helena. All these years you saw your life one way, and now suddenly you're faced with a new and different version of reality. To see the past changing before your eyes—what a shock!"

"Exactly. I feel dazed."

"There's also something very sad about your comments, Helena. It's sad how Billy, this vital, precious man, this lifelong friend, has been reduced to a diagnosis. And your entire youth with him—all those wonderful exciting experiences—also reduced to being 'nothing but,' nothing but an expression of mania. Perhaps he had some mania, but, from what you tell me, he seems so much more than just that label."

"I know, I know, but I can't get past that right now."

"Let me tell you what's going through my mind now. When you said that your entire youthful life with him was 'nothing but' mania, I shuddered a bit. I imagined applying this 'nothing but' approach to what's transpiring right now between you and me. I guess one might say that this is *nothing but* a commercial transaction and that I'm being paid for listening and responding to you. Or perhaps one might say that it helps me to feel stronger and more effective by helping you feel better. Or that I get life meaning from helping you attain meaning. And yes, all these things may be true. But to say therapy is 'nothing but' any of these things is so very far from the truth. I feel that you and I have encountered one another, that something real is occurring between us, that you're sharing so very much of yourself with me, and that I am moved and engaged by your words. I don't want us to be reduced, and I don't want Billy reduced. I like the thought of his miraculous midsummer smile. I envy your motorcycle ride through South America, and I'm sad at the thought of your taking all this away from yourself."

We ended, both of us tired and enlightened. She could reclaim her past and once again treasure her life with him. And, for my part, I had gained a new perspective on my longtime aversion to the act of diagnosis. During my training as a psychiatrist I often found the official diagnostic categories problematic. At case conferences, many of the consultants disagreed on the proper diagnosis of the patient presented, and I eventually grasped that the disagreements generally ensued not from practitioners' errors but from intrinsic problems in the diagnostic enterprise.

During my tenure as head of the Stanford inpatient ward I relied on diagnosis to inform decisions about effective pharmacological treatment. But in my psychotherapy practice over the last forty years with less-seriously disturbed patients, I have found the diagnostic process to be largely irrelevant, and I have come to believe that the contortions we psychotherapists must go through to meet the demands of insurance companies for precise diagnoses are detriments to both therapist and patient. In the diagnostic procedure we are not carving at the joints of nature. Diagnostic categories are invented and arbitrary: they are a product of committee vote and invariably undergo considerable revision with each passing decade.

But my meeting with Helena brought home to me that the chore of making a formal diagnosis is more than a simple nuisance. It may, in fact, *impede* our work by obscuring, even negating, the full-bodied, multidimensional individual facing us in our office. Billy was a victim of that process, and I was glad to play a part in restoring him to his former complexity and exuberance.

~ 10 ~

Creatures of a Day

Jarod entered my office and trudged straight to his chair without greeting me. I braced myself.

While staring out the window at strands of fleecy wisteria, he said, "Irv, I have a confession to make." He hesitated and then suddenly turned to face me directly to say, "This woman, Alicia . . . you remember my talking about her?"

"Alicia? We've spoken a great deal about Marie, of course, but no, I don't remember Alicia. Refresh my memory."

"Well, there is this other woman, Alicia, and the thing is . . . uh . . . Alicia also thinks I'm going to marry her."

"Whoa, I'm lost. Jarod, back up, and fill me in."

"Well, yesterday afternoon, when Marie and I met for our couples therapy session with your Patricia, the shit hit the fan. Marie began by opening her bag, pulling out a sheaf—a very large sheaf—of emails, highly incriminating emails, in which Alicia and I discussed marriage. So I decided I'd better fess up here today. I'd rather you hear this from me than from Patricia. Unless you've already talked to her."

I was stunned. In the year I had been meeting with Jarod, a thirty-two-year-old dermatologist, we had been focusing heavily on his relationship with Marie, his live-in partner for the last nine months. Though he claimed to love Marie, he balked at commitment. "Why should I," he said more than once, "offer up my *one and only life?*"

Up to now I had been under the impression that therapy was proceeding slowly but steadily. Jarod had been a philosophy major in college and had originally sought me out because he had read some of my philosophical novels and felt certain I would be the right therapist for him. In the first months of our work together he often resisted therapy through attempts to engage me in abstract philosophical discussions. However, in recent weeks, I saw less of that, and he seemed to have grown more serious and shared more and more of his inner self. Even so, Jarod's most pressing issue, his problematic relationship with Marie, remained unchanged. Knowing that it was futile to attempt couples work in an individual therapy setting, I had suggested a few weeks earlier that he and Marie see an excellent couples therapist, Dr. Patricia Johnson, whom today, out of the blue, he referred to as "my Patricia."

How to respond to Jarod's confession? Several directions beckoned: his crisis with Marie, his having led two women to believe he would marry them, his reaction to Marie's breaking into his email account, or his comment about "my Patricia" and the fantasies that underlay that. But all these things would have to wait a bit. I considered that my primary task just then was to attend to our therapeutic relationship. That always takes precedence.

"Jarod, let's go back and explore your very first comment: your statement about needing to make a confession. Obviously you've withheld some important things from our work, things that you speak of today only because you believe I'll hear about them from Patricia. From 'my Patricia.'"

Dammit, I shouldn't have added that last bit. I knew it would divert us, but it just popped out.

"Right, sorry about that Patricia crack. I don't know where it came from."

"Any hunches?"

"Not sure. I think it's just that you seemed so keen on her and so effusive in your praise of her ability. Plus she *is* drop-dead gorgeous."

"And so you thought there was something going on between Patricia and me?"

"Well, not really. I mean, for one thing, there *is* a big age difference. You said she was a student of yours about thirty years ago. I did some Internet research and learned she's married to a psychiatrist, another ex-student of yours . . . so . . . I mean . . . uh . . . tell you the truth, Irv, I don't know *why* I said that."

"Perhaps you may have wished it, wished that you and I were in collusion, that I, like you, was engaged in a problematic affair?"

"Preposterous."

"Preposterous?"

"Preposterous but . . . " Jarod nodded to himself a few times. "Preposterous, but probably true. I admit that when I walked in today, I felt exposed and alone, flapping in the breeze."

"So you wanted company? Wanted us to be co-conspirators?"

"I guess so. Makes sense. That is, it makes sense if you're psychotic. God, this is embarrassing. I feel like I'm about ten years old."

"I know this is uncomfortable, Jarod, but try to stay with it. I'm struck by your word 'confession.' What does it say about you and me?"

"Well, it says something about guilt. About something I've done that I hate to admit. I avoid telling you anything that would tarnish your view of me. I have a lot of respect for you . . . you know that . . . and I very much want you to continue to have a certain . . . uh . . . a certain *image* of me."

"What kind of image? What do you want Irv Yalom to think about Jarod Halsey? Take a moment and conjure up a scene in which I am attentive to your image."

"What? I can't." Jarod grimaced and shook his head as though to rid himself of a bad taste. "And anyway what are we doing now? This all seems off the mark. Why aren't we talking about the important stuff—my tight spot with Alicia and Marie?"

"That, too. Shortly. But humor me for a moment. Continue with our discussion of my image of you."

"Boy, I can really feel my unwillingness. This what you call 'resistance'?"

"In spades. I know this feels risky, but do you remember my telling you at our first meeting that it was important to take a risk each session? Now's the time! Try to risk it."

Jarod closed his eyes and turned his face toward the ceiling. "Okay, here goes . . . I see you in this office sitting there," he turned and, with eyes still shut, pointed in the direction of my desk at the opposite end of my office. "You're busy writing, and for some reason my image drifts into your mind. This what you mean?"

"Exactly. Don't stop."

"You close your eyes; you see my face in your mind and take a good long look at it."

"Good. Keep going. And now imagine my thoughts as I look at your face."

"You think, *Ah, there's Jarod. I see him . . .* " He seemed more relaxed as he sank into the fantasy task. "*Yes, that Jarod, what a fine fellow. So smart, so knowledgeable. A young man of unlimited promise. And so deep, so philosophically inclined.*"

"Keep going. What else am I thinking?"

"You're thinking, *What character he has, what integrity. . . . One of the best and brightest men I've ever seen . . . a man to be remembered.* That kind of stuff."

"Say more about how important it is that I have this image of you."

"Of *paramount* importance."

"It seems like it's more important for me to have this image of you than for me to help you change, which, after all, is the purpose of your consulting with me."

Jarod shook his head, resigned. "After what's gone down today, it's damned hard to refute that."

"Yes, if you withhold crucial information from me, like your relationship to Alicia, it *must* be so."

"Point taken. Believe me, the absurdity of my position is all too evident."

Jarod slumped in his chair, and we sat briefly in silence.

"Share what's passing through your mind."

"Shame. Mainly shame. I was ashamed to admit to you that I might not marry Marie when you . . . we . . . put in all that hard work together after Marie's cancer diagnosis and mastectomy."

"Keep going."

"I mean, what kind of a prick leaves a woman who has cancer? What kind of man betrays and abandons a woman because she has lost one of her tits? Shame. A lot of shame. And to make it worse, I'm a doctor: I'm supposed to care about people."

I began to feel some real sorrow for Jarod and spotted an impulse bubbling up in me to protect him from the wrath of his self-accusations. I wanted to remind him that his relationship to Marie was troubled long before she was diagnosed with cancer, but he was now in such decisional crisis that I feared saying anything he might interpret as advice. I have known too many patients in such a state who provoke others, including their therapist, to make their decision for them. In fact, it seemed likely to me that Jarod was covertly prodding Marie to make the decision to break off their relationship. After all, how did she discover those email messages? He must have unconsciously colluded with her; otherwise why hadn't he trashed and deleted that correspondence?

"And Alicia?" I asked. "Can you fill me in about you and her?"

"I've known her a few months. Met her at the gym."

"And?"

"Been seeing her a couple of times a week in the daytime."

"Oh, can you give me a little less information?"

Perplexed, Jarod looked up at me, noted my grin, and smiled. "I know, I know . . ."

"You must feel jammed up. This is an awkward and painful predicament. You come to me for help, but you're reluctant to speak openly."

"'Reluctant' is putting it delicately. I absolutely *hate* talking about this."

"Because of influencing the image I'll have of you in my mind?"

"Yes, because of that image."

I pondered Jarod's words for a few moments and then decided on an unorthodox strategy—one that I had rarely ever used in a course of therapy.

"Jarod, I happen to have been reading Marcus Aurelius recently, and I'd like to read you a few of his passages that seem pertinent to our discussion. Do you know his work?"

Jarod's eyes immediately filled with interest. He welcomed this respite. "Used to. I read his *Meditations* in a college course. I was a classics major for a while. But I haven't read him since."

I walked over to my desk to fetch my copy of *The Meditations of Marcus Aurelius* and started flipping through the pages. For the past few days I had been reading and highlighting passages because of an unusual interaction with another patient, Andrew. At our session the previous week Andrew had expressed, as he had done so many times before, his anguish at spending his life in a meaningless vocation. He worked as a high-salaried advertising executive and hated such meaningless goals as selling Rolls-Royce sedans to women wearing Galliano evening gowns. But he felt he had no choice: with advanced emphysema likely to shorten his productive work years, he needed the income to pay for his four children's college tuition and to care for his ailing parents. I surprised myself when I suggested to Andrew that he read *The Meditations of Marcus Aurelius*. I hadn't read Marcus Aurelius for many years, but I did recall that he and Andrew had something in common: Marcus Aurelius, too, had been forced into a vocation not of his own choosing. He would have preferred to be a philosopher, but he was the adopted son of a Roman emperor and was ultimately chosen to succeed his father. So instead of a life of thought and learning, he spent most of his adult years as an emperor fighting wars to protect the Roman Empire's borders. However, in order to maintain his own equanimity, Marcus Aurelius dictated, in Greek, his philosophical meditations to a Greek slave, who entered them into a daily journal meant only for the emperor's eyes.

After that session, it occurred to me that Andrew was so diligent he would, without doubt, do a close reading of Marcus Aurelius. Hence, I had to reacquaint myself immediately with *The Meditations*, and I spent much of my spare time in the previous week savoring that second-century Roman emperor's powerful, poignant words and preparing myself for the next session with Andrew, whom I was to see shortly after Jarod.

This was all in the back of my mind when I met with Jarod, and as he spoke of longing for his image to flicker forever in my brain, I grew persuaded that he, too, might be transformed by some of the ideas of Marcus Aurelius. At the same time I doubted my own inclinations: I had on many occasions observed that, whenever I read any of the great life-philosophers, I invariably sensed their relevance to many of the patients I was currently seeing and couldn't help citing some ideas or passages I had just stumbled on. Sometimes it was useful, but often not.

While Jarod waited, somewhat impatiently, I scanned the passages I had highlighted. "This will take just a few minutes, Jarod. I'm certain there are passages here that will be of value to you. Ah, here's one: 'Soon you will have forgotten all things: soon all things will have forgotten you.'

"And here's the one I was thinking of," I read aloud while Jarod closed his eyes, apparently in deep concentration. "'All of us are creatures of a day; the rememberer and the remembered alike. All is ephemeral—both memory and the object of memory. The time is at hand when you will have forgotten everything; and the time is at hand when all will have forgotten you. Always reflect that soon you will be no one, and nowhere.'

"And this one too: 'Swiftly the remembrance of all things is buried in the gulf of eternity.'"

I put down the book. "Any of these hit home?"

"What's the one starting with 'All of us are creatures of a day?'"

I reopened the book and read again:

All of us are creatures of a day; the rememberer and the remembered alike. All is ephemeral—both memory and the object of memory. The time is at hand when you will have forgotten everything; and the time is at hand when all will have forgotten you. Always reflect that soon you will be no one, and nowhere.

"Not sure why, but that one sent some shivers down my back," Jarod said.

BINGO! I was delighted. Just what I had hoped for. Maybe this was an inspired intervention after all. "Jarod, put other thoughts aside, and focus on that shiver. Give it a voice."

Jarod closed his eyes and appeared to sink into a reverie. After a few moments of silence, I again prodded him. "Reflect on this thought: *All of us are creatures of a day: the rememberer and the remembered alike.*"

Slowly Jarod, eyes still closed, responded. "Right now I have a crystal-clear memory of my first contact with Marcus Aurelius. . . . I was in Professor Jonathan Hall's class in my sophomore year at Dartmouth. He asked me for my reactions to Part 1 of *The Meditations*, and I posed a question that surprised and interested him. I asked, 'Who was the intended audience of Marcus Aurelius?' It is said that he never intended for others to read his words and that his words expressed things he knew already, so *to whom exactly was he writing?* I recall my question launching a long, interesting class discussion."

How annoying. How very annoying. How typical of Jarod to attempt to involve me in an interesting but distracting discussion. He was still trying to embellish my image of him. But over my year of work with him I had learned that it was best not to challenge him at times like this but, instead, to address his question directly and then gently guide him back to the issue.

"As far as I know, the scholars have felt that Marcus Aurelius was repeating these phrases to himself primarily as a daily exercise to bolster his resolve and to exhort himself to live a good life."

Jarod nodded. His body language signified satisfaction, and I continued, "But let's return to the particular passages I cited. You said you were moved by the one that began: 'All of us are creatures of a day; the rememberer and the remembered alike.'"

"Did I say I was moved? Perhaps I did, but for some reason it leaves me cold now. Honestly, right now, tell you the truth, I don't know *how* it applies to me."

"Maybe I can help by recalling the context for you. Let's see, ten, fifteen minutes ago, when you described the importance of my having a certain image of you, it occurred to me that certain Marcus Aurelius statements might be illuminating for you."

"But how?"

How irritating! Jarod seemed oddly obtuse today—ordinarily he had such a nimble mind. I considered commenting on his resistance but ruled that out because I had no doubt he would have a clever rebuttal and it would slow us down even more. I continued to plod along. "You place great importance on my image of you, so let me read the beginning of this one again: 'All of us are creatures of a day: the rememberer and the remembered alike.'"

Jarod shook his head, "I know you're trying to be helpful, but these stately pronouncements seem so off the mark. And so bleak and nihilistic. Yes, *of course* we are but creatures of a day. *Of course* everything passes in an instant. *Of course* we vanish without a trace. That's all pretty obvious. Who can deny it? But where's the help in that?"

"Try this, Jarod: keep in mind that phrase 'The time is at hand when all will have forgotten you,' and juxtapose that to the vast importance you place upon the persistence of your image in my mind, my very mortal, evanescent, eighty-one-year-old mind."

"But Irv, with all respect, you're not offering a coherent argument. . . . "

I could see Jarod's eyes sparkling with the prospect of an intellectual debate. He was in his element as he continued, "Look, I'm not arguing with you: I accept all is ephemeral. I have no pretense of being special or immortal. I know, like Marcus Aurelius, that eons of time have passed before I existed and that eons will go on after I cease to be. But how does that possibly bear on my wish for someone I respect, in other words, you, to think well of me during my brief time in the sun?"

Yikes! What a blunder to have tried this. I could hear the minutes clicking by. This discussion was eating up the whole session, and I felt pressed to salvage some part of our hour together. I always teach my students that, when you're in trouble in a session, you can always bail yourself out by calling on your ever-reliable tool, the "process check"—you halt the action and explore the relationship between you and the patient. I heeded my own advice.

"Jarod, can we stop for a moment and turn our attention to what's going on between you and me? How do you feel about the last fifteen minutes?"

"I think we're doing great. This is the most interesting session we've had for ages."

"You and I do share a delight in intellectual debate, but I have grave doubts that I'm being helpful to you today. I had hoped that some of these meditations would shed light on the importance of your desire for me to have a positive image of you in my mind, but I now agree with you that this was a hare-brained notion. I suggest we just drop it and use what little time remains today to address the crisis you're facing with Marie and Alicia."

"I don't agree it was harebrained. I think you were right on. I'm just too rattled now to think straight."

"Even so, let's go back to how things stand right now with you and Marie."

"I'm not sure *what* Marie is going to do. All this just happened this morning, and right after the session she had to get back to a research meeting in her lab. Or at least that's what she claims. Sometimes I think she fabricates excuses not to talk."

"But tell me this: What do you *want* to happen between the two of you?"

"I don't think it's up to me. After what's just happened, it's *her* call right now."

"Perhaps you don't *want* it to be your call. Here's a thought experiment: Tell me, if it *were* up to you, what would *you want* to happen?"

"That's just it. I don't know."

Jarod shook his head slowly, and we sat in silence for the last minutes of the hour.

As we prepared to end, I commented, "I want to underscore these last few moments. Keep them in mind. My question is: *What does it mean that you don't know what you want for yourself?* Let's start from that question next session. And, Jarod, here's one more thought to ponder during the week: I've got a hunch there's a connection, maybe a powerful connection, between your not knowing what you want and your powerful craving for your image to persist in my mind."

As Jarod stood to leave, I added, "You have a lot going on now, Jarod, and I'm not sure I've been helpful. If you're feeling pressed, call me, and we'll find a time to meet again this week."

I was not pleased with myself. In a sense, Jarod's confusion was understandable. He came to see me in extremis, and I responded by becoming professorial and pompous and reading him arcane passages from a second-century philosopher. What an amateurish error! What was I expecting? That simply reading Marcus Aurelius's words would, presto, magically enlighten and change him? That he would immediately realize that it was *his own* image of himself, his *own self-love*, that mattered, not *my* image of him? What was I thinking? I was embarrassed for myself and certain he left my office far more confused than when he had entered.

* * *

I had an hour-and-a-half break before my meeting with Andrew and put aside my thoughts about Jarod in order to read as much Marcus Aurelius as I could before seeing Andrew. The more I read, the more uncomfortable I grew because I had yet to come upon even one single mention of Marcus Aurelius expressing disgruntlement about his job and his longing for another life as a philosopher. Yet the very reason I had suggested to Andrew that he read the *Meditations* was that he and Marcus Aurelius shared a life predicament of being locked into a job they did not want. I began to dread our meeting: the prospect of yet another Marcus Aurelius fiasco loomed. My only hope was that

Andrew had been too busy to take my suggestion seriously and forgotten all about Marcus Aurelius.

But it was not to be. As Andrew jauntily entered my office, I spotted a well-bookmarked copy of Marcus Aurelius in his hand, and my heart sank. I braced myself as Andrew took his seat.

He began immediately: "Irv, this book," waving *The Meditations* at me, "has changed my life. Thank you, thank you, thank you. I cannot find the words to express my gratitude.

"Let me tell you what's happened since our last session. After I left your office, I stopped down the street at the City Lights bookstore and bought a copy of *The Meditations*, and the following morning I flew to New York to pitch our company for the account of a huge resort chain and gave, in my view, an excellent presentation in the evening. The next morning, just as I was boarding the plane to return home, I got an email on my iPhone from our new young CEO who had been present at my talk. He reminded me of a few additional important points I might have made in my pitch. Well, I totally lost it, and just before takeoff, I shot back an angry email telling him he didn't know what the fuck he was talking about and that he was free to search for someone who could do my job better. Fuming, I settled into my seat, slowly calmed down, and then spent the entire flight reading Marcus Aurelius. Five and a half hours later, I got off the plane a changed man. When I reread the CEO's email, I viewed it quite differently: it was basically a positive letter that politely made a couple of well-thought-out suggestions for my next talk. I phoned him, apologized, thanked him for his suggestions, and we've now started a great relationship."

"Quite a wonderful story, Andrew. Take me back to Marcus Aurelius. How did the book make such a difference?"

Andrew riffled through the heavily underlined pages for a couple of minutes and said, "This whole book is pure gold, but the particular passage that grabbed me was in Part 4. Here it is: 'Take away thy opinion, and then there is taken away the complaint, "I have been harmed." Take away the complaint, "I have been harmed," and the harm is taken away.'"

"Hmm, I don't recall that passage. Could you go over it again for me and tell me how it's been helpful?"

"He writes, 'Take away thy opinion, and then there is taken away the complaint, "I have been harmed." Take away the complaint, "I have been harmed," and the harm is taken away.' That's a core concept for the Stoics. I've been studying the text closely, and he makes that exact point in different words a number of times. For example, in Part 12 he writes: 'Jettison the judgment and you are saved. And who is there to prevent this jettison?' Or, only a few lines away, here's one I love: 'All is as thinking makes it so—and you control your thinking. So remove your judgments whenever you wish and then there is calm—as the sailor rounding the cape finds smooth water and the welcome of a waveless bay.'

"So," Andrew continued, "what he teaches me is that it is only your own perceptions that can harm you. Change your perceptions, and you eliminate the harm. Nothing from the outside can harm you because *you can only be harmed by your own vice.* The only way to respond to an enemy is not to be like him.

"Maybe this is simple, but it's an earth-shaping insight for me! Let me give you an example. Yesterday my wife was extremely stressed and harassed me endlessly for having misplaced a book that she needed. I could feel myself veering toward an explosion of anger toward her until I brought the words of Marcus Aurelius to mind: 'Remove the judgment "I have been harmed" and the harm is removed.' I began thinking of all the stress my wife was under—from a crisis at her workplace, from a dying father, from conflicts with our children—and then, instantaneously, the harm vanished, and I was full of compassion for my wife and sailing in the 'smooth water' of a 'waveless bay.'"

Oh what a pleasure it was to be with Andrew! As he taught himself, he taught me too. What a contrast to that vexing hour with Jarod. As Andrew spoke, I sat back and luxuriated in his words and those of Marcus Aurelius.

"Let me tell you something else I've learned," Andrew continued. "I've read a lot of philosophy in the past, but I now realize that I've always read for the wrong reasons. I read because of vanity. I read for the sake of being able to demonstrate my knowledge to others. This," Andrew held up his copy of *The Meditations*, "is the first authentic experience I've ever had with philosophy, my first realization that these wise old guys really had something important to say about life, about *my* life at this moment."

I finished the session full of humility and wonder. That elusive "aha" experience I had so futilely stalked in my hour with Jarod had, mirabile dictu, effortlessly materialized in my work with Andrew.

* * *

I didn't hear from Jarod during the week and was uncertain what to expect at our next session. He arrived right on time, greeted me, and began speaking immediately. "I have a lot to tell you. I almost phoned you a couple of times but managed to survive on my own. A shitload of stuff has gone down. Marie has gone. She left a one-sentence note: 'I need space to figure out my path and will be at my sister's house.' Remember you asked me last time how I would feel if she made the decision to leave? Well, that experiment has now been run, and I can tell you I don't feel released or liberated."

"What *do* you feel?"

"Mostly I feel sad. Sad for both of us. And restless and agitated. After I read her note, I didn't know what to do. I knew only that I had to get out of our apartment. There was just too much Marie there. So I asked a friend if I could stay at his small cottage in Muir Beach, packed an overnight bag, and spent a three-day weekend there with your Marcus."

"With *my* Marcus? That's a surprise! And? How did the weekend go for you?"

"Good. Maybe even *very* good. Sorry about last week. Sorry I was so dismissive and closed."

"You were in a state of shock last week, and, well, to put it mildly, my timing could've been better. So you say the weekend was 'maybe even *very* good'?"

"More so now. At the time it was painfully dreary. Just being alone like that was an unusual event. I don't think I've ever spent that much time alone just doing nothing except thinking about myself nonstop."

"Tell me about it."

"I think I was searching for a bare-bones retreat, something like Thoreau at Walden—though I read somewhere that Thoreau's mother packed him lunches for his retreats and took care of his dirty laundry. But in search of a real retreat, I made the ultimate sacrifice. I went there naked—no cell phone and no computer. I downloaded and printed out *The Meditations* before I left and made sure my partners would take all my patients' phone calls—though, as you probably know, dermatologists get few emergencies, which was one of my reasons for choosing the field. I felt strange without the Internet. I mean, if I wanted to find out about the weather, I actually had to stick my head out the window. So no structure for three days, aside from reading *The Meditations* slowly. And, oh yes, I had one other task: pondering your assignment, your thought experiment asking me to consider the connection between not knowing what I want and my craving that my image persist in your mind. I spent a big hunk of time on that."

Ah yes, that thought experiment. I had forgotten all about that, though I didn't wish to admit it. "So where are you in your thinking about that experiment?"

"I think I've found a solution. I'm pretty sure you were implying that I am lacking a self, that *I'm looking for me in you*, that my hollowness makes it impossible to identify my needs and my desires, and *that's* why I didn't or couldn't make a decision about Marie and forced her to make the decision—and *that's* why I craved some existence in your mind."

I was stunned. Speechless. For several moments I just looked up at Jarod's face. Did I know this man? Is this the same Jarod I'd met with for a year? His comments about the thought experiment were by far the most astute and honest comments about himself I had ever heard him utter. How to respond? As always, when I don't know what to say, I stuck to the truth.

"That thought experiment was a work in progress, Jarod. I didn't spend much time formulating it and had no definite answer in mind. It simply sprang up as we were ending our session, and I took a chance in telling it to you. My gut told me it might guide you to the right territory, and I think it succeeded. But let me ask something: I'm struck by your commenting that this is what you think *I* meant, what *I* thought. Can you own that yourself? What do *you* think?"

Jarod smiled, "Well, it's impossible to answer that, isn't it, because, if I lack a self, then who or what is the entity that's positing its own nonexistence?"

Oops, there he is again, the old Jarod, full of pratfalls and paradox. I didn't bite on this one, not for a second. "I don't recall that you've ever spoken before of this feeling of hollowness. That sounds important, and we should spend time exploring that. I'm struck by how much this weekend seems to have affected you. You seem so much more open, more willing to examine your own mind. Tell me, what was there in Marcus Aurelius that catalyzed this change?"

"I *knew* it! I *knew* you'd ask that. I've been asking myself the same question." Jarod opened his folder containing the pages of *The Meditations* and extracted a handwritten page. "Just before I came today I jotted down a few of the passages that made me shiver the most. I'll read them. They're in no particular order."

I have often wondered how it is that every man loves himself more than all the rest of men, but yet sets less value on his own opinion of himself than on the opinion of others.

If any man despises me, that is his problem. My only concern is not doing or saying anything deserving of contempt.

Never esteem anything as an advantage to you that will make you break your word or lose your self-respect.

"I like these very much, Jarod. And, indeed, they do speak straight to the issue we've been discussing—that the center of one's self-esteem and self-judgment should be within *yourself* rather than in the mind of another—that is, my image of you."

"Yes, I'm slowly getting the point. Here's another with a similar message:

"'If someone can prove me wrong and show me my mistakes in any thought or action. I shall gladly change. I seek the truth, which never harmed anyone: the harm is to persist in one's own self-deception and ignorance.'"

Jarod looked up from his page. "Sounds like these were written precisely for me. I have one last one. Shall I read it?"

I nodded. I love being read to, especially when the words are laden with wisdom.

"'Remember that this noble vintage is grape juice, and the purple robes of imperial office are sheep wool dyed with shell-fish blood. . . . Perceptions like that—latching onto things and piercing through them, so we see what they really are—that's what we need to do all the time—all through our lives when things lay claim to our trust—to lay them bare and see how pointless they are, to strip away the legend that encrusts them.'"

A dynamite passage! It made me shiver, too. And as he read, I thought of how this session was a mirror image of our last one: today he the reader and I the listener.

"I think I know your next question," said Jarod.

"And that is?"

"To be specific, to tell you exactly how these effected change."

"You're right on. Batting a thousand today. Can you take a crack at that one?"

"That seems so logical a question, but I can't really give you the answer. It just didn't work like that—it's not that I read a wise statement and suddenly changed."

Uh oh, here we were again. As usual, nothing was easy with Jarod. I longed for Andrew, who even without my prompting immediately pointed to the passage and the idea that changed everything for him. Why is Jarod so difficult? Why can't Jarod, *just once*, act like Andrew?

"What do you mean, Jarod, 'It didn't work like that'?"

"I wrote down passages that had shiver power—passages that shook me up. But I simply cannot make the leap and say *these particular words, these very thoughts*, changed me. It didn't work that way. There was no single epiphany. It's more global. It was the overall process."

"The overall process?"

"How to put it? Look, I'm blown away by this man's daily practice of self-scrutiny. *Every* morning he took himself more seriously than I have ever done *any morning* in my entire life. I've taken him inside of me as a model of how to live. Last week I raised the question, 'To whom was he writing?' I understand now.

It is obvious that his meditations are messages to his everyday self from that deep part of himself committed to live a good life. I think you implied that. Well, now *I* want to be able to do that. I admire him tremendously. What else can I say? Well, for one thing, this book, these meditations, make me see, really see, how truly fucked up I am. His meditations led me to understand that my whole life is wrong. I'm resolved to change. This week I'm going to level with both Marie and Alicia and tell them the truth: that I'm not ready for a committed relationship with anyone and that I have a ton of work to do on myself. I'm even reconsidering my professional life. I don't love what I'm doing, and as I once told you, I think I chose to specialize in dermatology because it was an easier life. I don't mean to knock my field—I mean that I'm not proud of my reasons for choosing it."

Jarod paused, and we sat in silence for several moments.

But I wanted to know more. Though I've been treating patients for fifty years, I continue to thirst for answers to the question of what really helps.

"Jarod, I understand how you were affected by the overall process, and I'll do all I can to encourage that process in the future. Nevertheless I still believe there may be some value in considering which of the specific meditations affected you. Can I take a look at the ones you just read to me?"

Jarod hesitated for a moment and then handed me the list.

I sensed his hesitation but decided not to comment on it. I knew what it meant: *I was out of tune with him.* My need to know is a good thing in that it fuels my interest in my patient, but sometimes, like that moment, it may be a bad thing in that I can't be satisfied with simply being present in the hour.

After scanning the list I commented, "I'm struck that several of the meditations you selected point to issues of virtue and integrity. They stress that harm can come to you only through your own vice."

"Yes, throughout the text Marcus Aurelius repeats that virtue is the only good, vice is the only bad. Again and again he makes the point that you, the core you, cannot be hurt if you maintain your virtue."

"So in other words he is showing you the path to creating a positive image of yourself."

"Yes, exactly. I heard that message loud and strong: if I'm virtuous and truthful, both to myself and to others, I will take pride in myself."

"And when you do that, it won't matter so much to you what image of you I have in *my* mind. One of my favorite psychiatrists, Karen Horney, wrote that if you want to feel virtuous, you must do virtuous things. It's a simple and venerable concept, right out of Marcus Aurelius, and Aristotle before him."

"Right. No more deception. Here with you or anywhere else."

"Let's start right now. We've still got a couple of minutes today. Let's use them to check into the feelings you've had about me today."

"Almost all positive. I know you're on my side and doing your best for me. The only moment when I felt slightly annoyed was when you pressed me about which words of Marcus Aurelius really helped. I felt you were asking me to distort my experience to satisfy your curiosity or corroborate your hunches or maybe to categorize my healing process."

"Point well taken, Jarod. Very well taken. It's a good observation and it is something I've got to work on."

* * *

Before my next patient I had ample time to think about Jarod and Andrew and the extraordinary drama I had witnessed. Once again I felt humbled by the endless complexity of the human mind and despaired at the vacuousness of my field's attempts to simplify and codify and generate how-to manuals to treat patients in some predesigned collective manner. Here were two patients who dived into a great-souled man's sea of wisdom, and each found benefit in a different way, in a way that neither I, nor any other mind, could possibly have predicted.

I wondered what this sea held for me as I approached my eighty-second birthday, full of life and passion and curiosity but saddened by the loss of so many people I had known and loved, at times mourning my lost youth, and distracted by my deteriorating scaffolding, my obstinate, creaking joints, my fading hearing and vision, and ever aware of the deepening dusk and relentless approach of the final darkness. I opened *The Meditations*, scanned the pages, and found the message meant for me:

Pass, then, through this little space of time in harmony with nature and end thy journey in contentment, just as an olive falls off when it is ripe, blessing nature who produced it, and thanking the tree on which it grew.

AFTERWORD

The most important thing I, or any other therapist, can do is offer an authentic healing relationship from which patients can draw whatever they need. We delude ourselves if we think that some specified action, be it an interpretation, suggestion, relabeling, or reassurance, is *the* healing factor.

Over and again the patients in these tales found benefit in ways I could not possibly have anticipated. One patient anoints me as witness to the fact that a significant person had deemed him significant. A patient's sense of fractured reality is mended by an unflinchingly authentic encounter with her therapist. Another grasps that real life is lived in the present moment. Another patient's life is changed by my referring him to a household organizer. A nurse is introduced to her better self. A muted writer finds her voice. A dying patient's last days are imbued with meaning when she serves as a pioneer of death for her friends and family. A patient, who is also a therapist, realizes that diagnosis may impair and distort understanding. A patient finds himself by emulating the practice of an ancient thinker. In each instance, I devised, or sometimes stumbled on, a unique approach for each patient that would not be found in any therapy manual. Because we may never know with precision *how* we have helped, we therapists have to learn to live comfortably with mystery as we accompany patients on their journey of self-discovery.

I write for those of you who have a keen interest in the human psyche and personal growth, for the many readers who will identify with the ageless existential crises depicted in these stories, and for individuals who contemplate entering therapy or are already in the midst of it. I hope these tales of reclamation will provide encouragement for those combatting their own demons.

It is also my great wish that the novice therapist will find value in this text. Its ten stories are meant to be teaching vehicles offering graphic lessons in psychotherapy that are not generally available in contemporary curricula. Most training programs today (often under pressure by accreditation boards or insurance companies) offer instruction only in brief, "empirically validated" therapies that consist of highly specific techniques addressing discrete diagnostic categories, such as depression, eating disorder, panic attacks, bipolar disease, addictions, or specific phobias. I worry that this current focus in education will ultimately result in losing sight of the whole person and that the humanistic, holistic approach I used with these ten patients may soon become extinct. Though research on effective psychotherapy continually shows that the most important factor determining outcome is the therapeutic relationship, the texture, the creation, and the evolution of this relationship are rarely a focus of training in graduate programs.

In these tales I hope to convey how a focus on the here and now can be used advantageously. Again and again I call attention to my bond with the patient: I do process checks; I inquire repeatedly about the state of our encounter during the current session; I ask if the patient has questions for me; I search for commentary on our relationship in dreams. In short, I never fail to place the highest priority on the development of an honest, transparent, helping bond between us.

I hope also that these stories will increase therapists' awareness of existential themes. In these ten stories I view my patients as suffering from maladies that defy traditional categorization. A young man attempts to ward off death terror through sexual vitality, an elderly man wrestling with the limitations of aging grasps for youthful spontaneity with its sense of unlimited horizons, a dying patient searches for meaning, a nurse ministers to others but cannot comfort herself, one person yearns for a better past, and another attempts to compensate for his missing sense of self by planting his banner in my memory.

Far more patients grapple with existential issues than is generally thought. The patients in these stories deal with anxiety about death, about the loss of loved ones and the ultimate loss of oneself, about how to live a meaningful life, about coping with aging and diminished possibilities, about choice, about fundamental isolation. To offer help, therapists need a keen sensibility to existential issues and must reach a formulation of what ails and what must be done that differs radically from formulations offered by clinicians of other orientations.

NOTE TO THE READER

In the service of confidentiality, I have heavily disguised each patient's identity and, on a few occasions, introduced parts of other patients' histories or, occasionally, fictional scenes into a story. I showed every living patient the final draft of his or her story and obtained approval and written permission for publication. Though Paul ("The Crooked Cure") and Astrid ("Show Some Class for Your Kids") had died long before, I disguised their stories and identities beyond recognition; I believe they would have been pleased for their experiences to be used to teach others. Ellie ("Get Your Own Damn Fatal Illness") died as I was writing her story, but she approved my description of the project, was pleased I would be using her words, and insisted only that I use her real name.

ACKNOWLEDGMENTS

My son, Ben Yalom, the primary editor for this book, negotiated with grace the perils of editing his fathers writing and was enormously helpful at all stages of this work. And my wife, Marilyn, always my toughest critic, provided assistance from start to finish. My literary agent, Sandy Dijkstra, was, as always, a treasure. My heartfelt thanks also to my many friends and colleagues who read one or more of these stories and offered useful suggestions: Svetlana Shtukareva, David Spiegel, Robert Berger, Herb Kotz, Ruthellen Josselson, Hans Steiner, Randy Weingarten, and all the members of the Pegasus writing group.